The Self as Agent

This is the first volume of
Professor John Macmurray's Gifford Lectures
given under the title

THE FORM OF THE PERSONAL

THE SELF AS AGENT

by

JOHN MACMURRAY
M.C., M.A., LL.D.

FABER AND FABER LIMITED

London

First published in 1957
by Faber and Faber Limited
24 Russell Square, London, W.C.1
First published in this edition 1969
Printed in Great Britain by
Latimer Trend & Co Ltd Whitstable
All rights reserved

SBN 571 09244 6

Contents

Introductory

This volume contains the substance of the Gifford Lectures delivered in the University of Glasgow during the Spring term of 1953. The second series of these lectures, delivered the following Spring under the title *Persons in Relation*, will be published in due course. The general subject of the lectures was dictated by a double criticism of our philosophical tradition. The traditional point of view is both theoretical and egocentric. It is theoretical in that it proceeds as though the Self were a pure *subject* for whom the world is *object*. This means that the point of view adopted by our philosophy is that of the Self in its moment of reflection, when its activity is directed towards the acquirement of knowledge. Since the Self in reflection is withdrawn from action, withdrawn into itself, withdrawn from participation in the life of the world into contemplation, this point of view is also egocentric. The Self in reflection is self-isolated from the world which it knows. This theoretical and egocentric character of our philosophy is not doctrinal. It is a presupposition, generally unconscious, implicit in philosophical procedures. It is quite compatible with voluntarism. Fichte, for instance, begins from the assertion, 'In the beginning was the Act'. But this 'act' turns out to be an *act of consciousness*, and its objective the theoretical and egocentric one of complete self-consciousness.

My purpose has been to challenge both these presuppositions. Against the assumption that the Self is, at least primarily, a 'knowing subject', I have maintained that its subjecthood is a derivative and negative aspect of its agency. This corresponds to the fact that most of our knowledge, and all our primary knowledge, arises as an aspect of activities which have practical, not theoretical objectives; and that it is this knowledge, itself an aspect of action, to which all reflective theory must refer. Against the assumption that the Self is an isolated individual, I have set the view that the Self is a *person*, and that personal existence is *constituted* by the relation of persons.

The present volume is concerned with the former of the two issues, and so with the Self as Agent. The question of the inter-relation of selves—the proposal to substitute the 'You and I' for the solitary 'I' of the philosophical tradition—has been re-served, in order to facilitate exposition, for the second volume. This method has disadvantages, and may even be misleading, if the incompleteness of the first volume is forgotten. It may there-fore be desirable to say at once that the agent-self which will be the subject of our present discussions is a logical abstraction, and can exist only as a community of personal agents.

The misunderstanding, however, against which it is most important to guard, touches the purpose, or the philosophical function, of these lectures. Because they range, in a systematic fashion, over every general aspect of human experience, they may suggest that what is offered is a new philosophical system. This is not the case. Unlike many of my contemporaries, I have no objection to system-making; I consider it, indeed, in its proper place, a necessary part of the philosophical enterprise. Most systems of philosophy, indeed, are the product, not of the genius of the original thinkers to whom they are ascribed, but of the industry of their commentators. But there are system-builders among the great philosophers. Aristotle, Aquinas, Hegel are examples. Their function is to give a definitive and systematic expression to a process of thought which has been unfolding itself over a period of history. At the beginning of such processes stand the pioneers, thinkers like Pythagoras or Descartes, whose function it is to reject current presuppositions and to establish a new point of view, with new assumptions. The process itself, which unites these two extremes, consists in the gradual discovery of the implications and consequences of the new point of view. The present work is a pioneering venture. It seeks to establish a point of view. Its purpose, therefore, is formal and logical—to construct and to illustrate in application the form of the personal.

A new philosophical form cannot be established by demonstration. It can only be exhibited and illustrated in use. It is possible to show the need for new formal construction by a critical analysis of the philosophical tradition. The forms in actual use—at present the mechanical (or mathematical) form and the organic (or dialectical)—can be shown to prove inadequate to their function. The analysis can be used to indicate the *locus* of this inadequacy, and so to suggest the starting-point of a new construction. Further, the analysis of this starting-point can be made to yield the form which it implies and the presuppositions which this form carries with it. But the verification can only be undertaken through an attempt to apply the new form over the whole field which it must cover. The function of a philosophical form is to exhibit the unity of human experience as a whole, in all its general aspects, both theoretical and practical. To verify it is to show that it is capable of doing so. This explains the appearance of system-building. It has been necessary to consider each major field of human activity, both practical and reflective, in systematic order, from the new point of view, and to offer at least the suggestion of a theory in each which might be compatible with the new form. But this process has been carried only to the point where the application of the form has been sufficiently illustrated. What has been attempted is to indicate, in each field, the modification of traditional theory that seems to be required. The paramount interest has remained the same throughout—to clarify the form and to exhibit its philosophical adequacy.

It goes without saying that the suggestions I have made, in this or the other field, are intended to be serious contributions to the developing content of philosophical theory. I hope that when they are worked out to the point at which the difficulties and doubts to which they must give rise become apparent they will be found capable of withstanding criticism; if not in all cases, at least in some. My confidence, however, is severely qualified by a knowledge of the inherent difficulty of the task. It is one thing to discover the presuppositions underlying a historic tradition, and to recognize that they are no longer tenable. It is quite another, if that tradition is one's own, to track down all the effects of those presuppositions upon the body of belief and opinion which one has inherited. The influence of the old assumptions is pervasive and unformulated. It is not possible, even if it were desirable, to empty one's mind completely and start afresh in a condition of intellectual innocence. It is only to be expected, therefore, that I have carried over much from the old order that should have been left behind, and that my tentative theorizing will be found liable, at many points, to the objection that it still presupposes what it purports to reject. Yet even should this prove the case in a much larger measure than I hope and expect, the main object of these lectures would remain unaffected. The form of the personal would still have been exhibited and the possible range of its application would have been illustrated, even if all the particular applications had gone awry through the intrusion of attitudes and assumptions which ought to have been excluded.

This nagging doubt has, however, a more cheerful aspect. Criticisms of these applications which remain, whether consciously or unconsciously, within the presuppositions of the traditional philosophy, and which depend upon the logical forms which I have rejected, have no force. For critics also the formal issue is paramount.

So far as the nature of the subject-matter would allow I have sought to employ the methods and the terminology which are usual in abstract and formal philosophical analysis. But it is in accordance with the general thesis that the abstract theoretical discussion has a concrete and practical reference and that this, too, should be expressed. The simplest expression that I can find for the thesis I have tried to maintain is this: All meaningful knowledge is for the sake of action, and all meaningful action for the sake of friendship.

I am glad to have this opportunity to express my gratitude to the University of Glasgow for the invitation to prepare these lectures, and to colleagues and friends in that University for the kindness and hospitality which made their delivery a delight. I also owe a debt to my philosophical colleagues in Edinburgh for their helpful criticism and encouragement. In particular I should like to thank Dr. Frederick Broadie for checking the manuscript and compiling the index.

Edinburgh,　　　　　　　　　　　　　　　　JOHN MACMURRAY
　September 1956.

CHAPTER ONE

The Crisis of the Personal

'The Form of the Personal' was the subject which I chose for the two series of Gifford Lectures which were delivered in the University of Glasgow in the Spring of 1953 and of 1954. For this choice I had two main reasons; the first, that it is, in my judgement, the emergent problem for contemporary philosophy; the second, that it directs attention to that aspect of our common experience from which religion springs, and is in this respect appropriate to the purpose of the Gifford foundation. For it is characteristic of religion that it behaves towards its object in ways that are suitable to personal intercourse; and the conception of a deity is the conception of a personal ground of all that we experience. If then human reason, unaided by revelation, can contribute anything to theology, it is through a philosophical analysis of the personal that we should expect this to be brought to light.

I must treat this theme as a philosopher, for that is my only competence. But here I am embarrassed by the widespread doubt whether a natural theology is at all possible; whether indeed such a branch of knowledge properly exists. If it can be made possible, then it must be a part of philosophy; yet among philosophers today the most prevalent view would seem to be that there can be no natural theology, but at most a philosophy of religion. If we disregard philosophies which are grounded in a dogmatic theology on the one hand or in a dogmatic atheism on the other, it would be fair to say that for the most part the debate about the status of theological beliefs turns upon the validity or illusoriness of specifically religious experience. But this would appear to rule out, by implication, the possibility of any natural theology. For by this term is meant, as I understand it, a theology which is based upon our common human experience of the world, and which requires no help from special experiences of a peculiarly religious kind. It must be discoverable by reason alone, without the need to have recourse to faith.

This philosophical tendency to discount the possibility of a natural theology is confirmed by the most vigorous and challenging of contemporary developments in theology itself. The Theology of Crisis has stressed the complete otherness of God to a point where the notion that reason could even suggest the divine becomes evidently irrational, and the idea of a natural theology itself unnatural. So, in our time, philosophers and theologians tend to unite, it would seem, in agreement that religion must rest upon its own evidence, and that any knowledge we may have of the divine must be revealed to us in 'religious' experiences whose validity is evidenced by an inner conviction of their authenticity in those to whom they are granted.

When both philosophy and theology tend in this matter to recognize an impassable gulf between faith and reason, it would seem that the philosopher, who must stand by reason, should conclude to atheism. He cannot admit, as premisses of his argument, any special experiences, religious or other, whose validity is at all questionable. He must start from common experience at its most universal and its most ordinary; and his procedure must be by rational analysis and rational inference. At no point can he admit as evidence any experience which is radically heterogeneous with this commonplace starting-point, and which could point to no evidence in common experience to bear witness for it. Such a disparity between normal and religious experience would convict of unreality the abnormality of the latter. If there is no point at which faith and reason can meet, then it is unreasonable to accept the deliverances of faith, and atheism is the reasonable conclusion.

It is undeniable that the historic development of modern philosophy has moved in this direction. In its beginnings it is unquestioningly theist, and confident of its capacity to demonstrate the existence of God. Even Hobbes and Machiavelli profess a religious belief which we should consider hardly compatible with their modes of thought. This early confidence has gradually faded; and in the end has been replaced by the conviction that any attempt to sustain religion by philosophical reasoning is to be suspected of special pleading. The long argument which Descartes initiated has moved decisively in the direction of atheism.

It may be said that this is only history, and that it merely reflects the progressive decline of the authority of religion in our civilization during the modern period. There is truth in this. Yet the history of our philosophy is our social history at its most serious, its most reflective and its most logical. May not the failure of reason to sustain the argument for religion be in turn part of the explanation of the decline of faith? I do not wish to argue these issues now. I shall content myself, at this stage, with expressing my belief that the more closely modern philosophy keeps to its programme, and the more purely objective its procedure becomes, the more inevitable is the atheism of its conclusion. Within the limits of its assumptions no other result is permissible.

Yet I cannot accept the conclusion, in spite of its logical necessity; and that I am not alone in this seems to be shown by the reluctance of so many competent philosophers explicitly to draw it. When I forget the course of the argument, I find the conclusion unreasonable, and indeed *prima facie* incredible. I do not mean that atheism in itself is *prima facie* irrational. But the view that there is no path from common experience to a belief in God; that religion rests upon some special and extraordinary type of experience apart from which it could not arise—this seems to me hardly credible. For if it were true we should expect to find (should we not?) that religion developed late in the history of culture, and sporadically, under the influence of

unusual conditions of life. Interest in religion, one would imagine, would be confined to special types of men, with abnormal
and possibly somewhat deranged sensibilities; and we should
expect also to find no connexion between religion and more
usual forms of reflective activity. Yet the opposite of all this is
the case. Religion is the original, and the one universal expression of our human capacity to reflect; as primitive and as
general as speech. It is atheists and agnostics who have been
exceptional and abnormal. They have indeed constituted a very
small minority at all times, although their numbers have tended
to increase in epochs of social dissolution. So far, too, from being
heterogeneous with other aspects of culture, and resting upon
abnormal experience which contrasts with our common awareness of the world, religion is the source from which the various
aspects of human culture have been derived; and the belief in a
radical disparity between philosophy and theology is an exceptional and recent phenomenon.

These considerations do nothing, of course, to prove the
validity of religious belief; but they do make it unlikely that our
common, primary experience provides no evidence tending to
support it. If then modern philosophy fails to find any, may it
not be because it works within limits which exclude the evidence
from its consideration; or that it rests upon assumptions, so
familiar perhaps that they have lapsed from consciousness,
which require scrutiny and modification? This is the view, at
least, to which my own reflection has led me, and which determines the method which I shall pursue in the discussion of my
theme. Quite apart from all specifically theological questions,
I believe that the emergent problem of contemporary philosophy necessitates a revision of traditional assumptions; and that
when this revision has been made the direction of the argument
will be so altered that it will tend thereafter to a theistic conclusion.

Since I am of this mind, I propose to put aside any discussion
of religion until it arises in the natural development of the argument, and to proceed, in a purely philosophical manner, upon

an inquiry which arises, within the normal field of modern philosophy, from the analysis and interpretation of common human experience. I shall invite attention to what I take to be the emergent problem of contemporary philosophy, and initiate the criticism of current assumptions which it requires. If this leads, as I believe it does, to modifications of outlook which require a theistic conclusion I shall have fulfilled the intentions of the founder of the Gifford lectureship, though indirectly, yet in the best way that is open to me.

I have referred to the form of the personal as the emergent problem of contemporary philosophy, and this requires both to be explained and to be justified. For it is far from being the case that this is the problem with which philosophy is particularly concerning itself at present. What is meant is rather that the historical situation in which we find ourselves presents us with a philosophical problem for solution, and that this problem concerns the form of the personal. The decisive questions of serious philosophy are never determined at random. They have their origins in a historical necessity, not in the chance interests of a particular thinker. Philosophy aims at a complete rationality. But the rationality of our conclusions does not depend alone upon the correctness of our thinking. It depends even more upon the propriety of the questions with which we concern ourselves. The primary and the critical task is the discovery of the problem. If we ask the wrong question the logical correctness of our answer is of little consequence.

There is of necessity an interplay, in all human activities, between theory and practice. It is characteristic of Man that he solves his practical problems by taking thought; and all his theoretical activities have their origins, at least, in his practical requirements. That they also find their meaning and their significance in the practical field will command less general assent; yet it is, in my belief, the truth of the matter, and one of the major theses to be maintained here. Activities of ours which are purely theoretical, if this means that they have no reference to our practical life, must be purely imaginary—exercises of phantasy which are not even illusory unless we relate them to the practical world by a misplaced belief. The truth or falsity of the theoretical is to be found solely in its reference to the practical.

This may be what is intended by the assertion current in some philosophical circles that the meaning of a proposition is the method of its verification. If so, I can have no quarrel with this doctrine. I should like to be sure, however, that it is recognized that the method of verification with which the physical sciences have made us familiar is not the only way in which the theoretical can refer to the practical. There are other modes of verification; indeed, if there were not, the scientific mode would itself be invalid and indeed impossible. But this is not the moment to enter into these issues in detail. We must limit ourselves to what seems reasonable at a first inspection. For every inquiry must start from what is the case *prima facie*. We know how large a part of our thinking is concerned with the solution of practical issues. In such cases it is obvious to everyone that the reference is to practical behaviour, and that conclusions which have no bearing upon the solution of our practical problems are without significance. The theoretical question is posed by the practical situation; for that very reason the significance and the verification of the theoretical conclusion lie in the practical field. Indeed the theoretical result, if it is meaningful at all, is the solution of a *practical* problem. If then, as seems indubitable, all theoretical problems have their ultimate, if not their immediate, origin in our practical experience it seems reasonable to expect that all must find their ultimate meaning in a reference to the practical. It may indeed turn out otherwise. There may be generated, by the instigation of practical experience, a set of theoretical activities which have their meaning in themselves and require no practical reference to sustain or to validate them. But it would be a methodological error to assume this from the start.

This does not mean, however, that the reference of theoretical to practical activities is always direct or obvious. Nor does it mean that in our reflection we can or should always be aware of the practical reference. It does not justify a pragmatic theory of truth nor suggest that we should not seek knowledge for its own sake. The disinterested pursuit of the truth may be, and, I am convinced, is in fact, a condition of the practical efficacy of reflection. The inner life of the spirit is not merely technological: it is not condemned to a servitude to practical ends which are set for it without its knowledge or consent. The essential reference of theoretical to practical activities does not involve the control of theory by practice. It consists even more significantly in the control of practice by theory; in the determination, through reflection, of the ends of action. All that is contended for is this, that there is a necessary relation between our theory and our practice; that the activities of reflection can never be totally unrelated to practical life; that it is always legitimate to ask, of any theory which claims to be true, what practical difference it would make if we believed it. It may often be difficult to answer this question; but if the correct answer were that it would make no difference at all, then the theory would be a mere exercise of phantasy, neither true nor false, but meaningless.

I have laboured a truism because I am thinking primarily of philosophy. For here, if anywhere, it might seem to be true that we are involved in a theoretical activity which has no practical reference. This I am concerned to deny. In philosophy, indeed, the reference to practice is indirect and remote throughout much of its range. Here too it is especially important that the question of the ultimate reference to practice should not obsess the thinker, or control the processes of his reflection. But it is also in philosophy that the ultimate reference of theory to practice is most decisive and far-reaching. It is not for nothing that some have held that a philosophy is a way of life; or that common tradition conceives the philosopher as a man of a balanced temper, who meets fortune or disaster with equanimity. Our western philosophy began with the breakdown of a way of life in ancient Greece, which posed the question 'What should we do?' If it has found itself driven to dwell almost exclusively with the sister question 'How can we know?' it remains true that this question is incomplete in itself; and that the complete question, in the end, is 'How can we know what we should do?'

Now action is inherently particular; and therefore questions of the form 'What shall I do?' have a historic reference. They cannot be answered without regard to the circumstances in which we have to act. Since philosophy, like all modes of reflection, involves, however indirectly, a practical reference, it is not exempt from the changes of circumstance. However eternal may be the problems to which it seeks a solution, philosophy has a history, and this is essential, not accidental to it. This reference to history has a double aspect. There is a historical process within philosophy which preserves a continuity of development from one age to its successor, and which calls for historical study and understanding. But also philosophy is itself one element in the social process, and is linked in numerous and essential ways to the other aspects of historical development. One can never fully understand, and may easily misunderstand a past philosophy, if one does not also understand in some measure the practical history of the era of its origin.

Instead of saying that a philosophy is a way of life, it would be better to say that any way of life implies a philosophy. For if it is a way of life at all it must be a relatively satisfactory adjustment to Reality, exhibiting a systematic structure, and, to a considerable degree, a consistency of direction. Any effort to give reflective expression to such a way of life must formulate a system of beliefs about the nature of the world and a system of priorities in valuation. The expression of a social tradition provides, therefore, if not a philosophy, at least the raw material for one. To achieve such a formulation would in itself provide a task of immense magnitude and difficulty if it had to begin from scratch, as it were. But the individual philosopher finds the tradition which he shares already formulated, if not analytically systematized. And since the formulation is never fully satisfactory, reflection will find, and will tend to concentrate attention upon the inconsistencies and incoherences which are involved and which reflect, in their fashion, the strains and stresses arising from a practical inadequacy. The philosophical effort to achieve consistency implies then, even if it does not intend, a modification of the way of life itself which would eliminate what is practically unsatisfactory in its working. We see here the practical ground of the two conditions that any valid philosophy must satisfy—a theoretical consistency and a comprehensive adequacy. The need for consistency is obvious. The demand for adequacy arises from this, that the effort to overcome any practical maladjustment in a way of life may, by its success, generate even more serious difficulties in other departments.

That there is such an interrelation, indirect enough and largely unconscious, between philosophical theory and social processes of a more empirical kind, is evident from any study of the history of philosophy which looks for it. The philosophy of any historical period reflects the life of the period even more evidently than does its art. One aspect of this to which I would draw attention is particularly obvious. The breakdown of a social tradition involves a break in the continuity of philosophical development, and the more revolutionary is the social crisis, the more thorough is the break in the philosophical tradition. One might instance the change in ancient philosophy which marks the fall of the city-state and the rise of the empires; or in modern philosophy in the transition from the mediaeval world. In such revolutionary periods philosophy responds to the practical transformation of the way of life by a radical transformation of its central problem. A new starting-point is discovered and a new era of reflection begins. So long as a way of life remains viable, the philosopher works within a framework of thought which in its general structure and in its general concepts remains stable. His problems are problems of relative detail, and he finds them set for him by difficulties in the theoretical field itself. Their relation to the practical problems of his society is indirect and need not be noticed. But with a break in tradition this is no longer the case. His criticism no longer touches this or that inconsistency or inadequacy in a continuing tradition, but the basis of the tradition itself. He must find a new starting-point; and his success depends on the discovery of the emergent problem for philosophy in his own time.

Perhaps I have said enough to suggest a *prima facie* case for the view that there is a necessary relation between philosophy and social practice. My immediate purpose falls short of this. It is to explain what is meant by saying that the form of the personal is the emergent problem for contemporary philosophy. That we are living through a period of revolutionary change is already a commonplace. We are all aware of this, though we may differ in our estimate of the depth and the extent of the transformation that has already occurred or that is inevitable as we go forward. To me it seems certain that the scale of change must dwarf the transformation of medieval into modern Europe. For that historic revolution fell within the development of Western Christendom, and rested upon a deeper continuity of Graeco-Roman tradition; while ours arises from the incompatibility of age-old ways of life in a world already largely forced into unity at the economic and technological levels. The European tradition, not to speak of its national variations, is now only one factor in a conflict of traditions which must achieve a practical compatibility if civilization is to maintain itself.

But these are large speculations upon which we shall not enter. We need only recognize the break with tradition which is apparent in all fields in our own society—in religion and morals, in politics and economics, and in the arts. In such circumstances we should expect to find a break in the continuity of philosophical development, a radical criticism of traditional philosophy and a search for new ways and new beginnings. And this we do find. We need only think of such developments as phenomenology, logical empiricism or existentialism to realize that new modes of philosophy are being created and spreading rapidly, which stand in strong contrast

26

with the main stream of traditional thought. The first of these is confessedly an effort to start afresh where Descartes started, but employing a catharsis of the mind to remove prejudice and achieve an innocence of immediate vision for whatever can be object for thought. Logical empiricism, armed with a high-powered analytic technology, is concerned to make an end of all metaphysics, and to include under metaphysics most of what has traditionally been considered the substance of philosophical doctrine. Its main interest in the past is to show how it was constantly led, not into error, but into meaningless debate by failure to perform the only proper task of philosophy, the logical analysis of language. Existentialism, on the other hand, has so altered the focus of attention, and so largely turned its back upon the established methods of procedure that many have doubted its claim to be a philosophical discipline at all.

These two contemporary forms of philosophy, logical empiricism and existentialism, represent, it would seem, opposite reactions to the breakdown of the tradition. They are united in the extremity of their difference, not merely by their negative attitude to the philosophical past, but if I mistake not, by a common conviction from which both arise. I may express this roughly by saying that both rest upon the decision that the traditional method of philosophy is incapable of solving its traditional problems. But whereas the logical empiricists discard the problems in order to maintain the method, the existentialists relinquish the method in wrestling with the problems. So the latter achieve a minimum of form; the former a minimum of substance. The logical empiricists are content to elaborate the subtleties of formal analysis—and often with the beauty of genius; so far as the substantial problems go, they use their formalism to erect notices on every path which say 'No road this way!' For all the roads that do not lead to the impassable bogs of metaphysics belong to the special sciences. The existentialists, determined to grapple with the real problems—and their sensitiveness to the darkness of human despair leads them to discover the emergent problem of our time—find no formal analysis that is adequate to the task. They are constrained to quit the beaten track; to wallow in metaphor and suggestion; to look to the drama and the novel to provide an expression, albeit an aesthetic expression, for their discoveries.

Where is the way forward? Do we go along with one of these contemporary schools of thought? Or should we count them as aberrations engendered by the stress and sickness of our age, and hold to the beaten paths of traditional thought? My own answer to this decisive question is as follows. We *cannot* keep to the old ways. The tradition is broken, and cannot be re-established. It is true, as the new movements imply, that the traditional methods cannot answer the traditional questions. Form and matter, in philosophy, have parted company. Then what of the new modes? Phenomenological analysis is a useful device. We can be grateful for it, and use it when we find it helpful. But if it is taken as more than this; if it means that we go back to Descartes and the modern starting-point and do properly what we have so far done poorly, we must answer that there is no going back. History does not repeat itself. Yet when I turn to choose between the other two schools, I find I can accept neither. To the logical empiricists I find I must say this: 'Philosophy, like any branch of serious reflective inquiry, is created and defined by its problems; and its problems are not accidental, but necessary; grounded in the nature of human experience. If I find that my method of attempting to answer them is unsuccessful, if it fails even to discover a meaning in them, then I must conclude that there is something wrong with the method, and seek a better one. To discard the problems in order to retain the method; to seek for problems which the method *could* solve, would be neither serious nor reasonable.' To the existentialists I should say this: 'Philosophy, as you would agree, is an intellectual discipline. It is therefore necessarily formal and must work through concepts which seek for clarity and exact definition both in themselves and in their systematic interrelation. It is right to hold firmly to the substantial problems, however metaphysical and elusive, which form the centre of gravity of the philosophic enterprise. It is an important contribution to the progress of the enterprise to trace them to their origins in the strains and stresses of the personal life. But if this results in the dissolution of the formal structures of traditional philosophy, what is required is the search for a new form which shall be not less but more logical and intellectual than the inadequate forms that have to be discarded.' We may sum up this estimate of these two emergent philosophical tendencies in a sentence, even though, like all such judgements, it must need qualification in detail. Existentialism has discovered, with sensitiveness of feeling, that the philosophical problem of the present lies in a crisis of the personal: logical empiricism recognizes it as a crisis of logical form and method. Both are correct, and both are one-sided. The cultural crisis of the present is indeed a crisis of the personal. But the problem it presents to philosophy is a formal one. It is to discover or to construct the intellectual form of the personal.

I need hardly labour to convince you that the cultural crisis of our time is a crisis of the personal. This is too general a conclusion of those who look deeper into the troubles of our society than the superficial level of organizational strain, whether economic or political. I need only refer to two aspects of the situation, both very familiar, in order to make clear what I mean by a crisis of the personal. One of these is the tendency towards an apotheosis of the state; the other the decline of religion. The two are intimately connected; since both express a growing tendency to look for salvation to political rather than to religious authority. The increasing appeal to authority itself reflects a growing inability or unwillingness to assume personal responsibility. The apotheosis of political authority involves the subordination of the personal aspect of human life to its functional aspect. The major social revolutions of our time all wear this livery, whether they are fascist or communist in type. The justification offered by the democracies for resistance to the death against both is the same, that they rest upon a philosophy which sacrifices the personal values, and so the personal freedom of men to the exigencies of political and economic expediency. At this level, the crisis of the personal is the crisis of liberalism, which was an effort, however ambiguous, to subordinate the functional organization of society to the personal life of its members. Yet nothing could be more revealing of the depth of the crisis we are facing than one fact. Communism rests upon a criticism of liberal democracy. Liberalism, it maintains, contradicts itself. While it stands, in theory, for human freedom, in practice it is a defence of human exploitation. Communism set out to resolve this contradiction by abolishing exploitation and realizing freedom in social practice. The declared intention was to achieve a form of society in which the government of men would give place to the administration of things. Yet its own practice, we see, defeats its intention, and leads to an apotheosis of the State and to an organized and efficient exploitation of its citizens. In communist practice the personal is subordinated to the functional to a point at which the defence of the personal becomes itself a criminal activity.

The decline of religious influence and of religious practice in our civilization bears the same significance. Such a decline betrays, and in turn intensifies, a growing insensitiveness to the personal aspects of life, and a growing indifference to personal values. Christianity, in particular, is the exponent and the guardian of the personal, and the function of organized Christianity in our history has been to foster and maintain the personal life and to bear continuous witness, in symbol and doctrine, to the ultimacy of personal values. If this influence is removed or ceases to be effective, the awareness of personal issues will tend to be lost, in the pressure of functional preoccupations, by all except those who are by nature specially sensitive to them. The sense of personal dignity as well as of personal unworthiness will atrophy, with the decline in habits of self-examination. Ideals of sanctity or holiness will begin to seem incomprehensible or even comical. Success will tend to become the criterion of rightness, and there will spread through society a temper which is extraverted, pragmatic and merely objective, for which all problems are soluble by better organization. In such conditions the religious impulses of men will attach themselves to the persons who wield political power, and will invest them with a personal authority over the life of the community and of its members. The state is then compelled to perform the functions of a church (for which by its nature it is radically unfitted) and its efforts to do so will produce, the more rapidly the more whole-hearted they are, a crisis of the personal. If we remember that history has brought us to a point where we must think of human society as a whole, and not limit our outlook to the confines of our own nation, there must be few who will fail to recognize, whether they welcome it or recoil from it, that we are involved in such a crisis.

It may be asked, however, whether this has any relevance for philosophy. To answer this doubt requires a reference to the broad outline of the history of modern philosophy. For brevity's sake, and because my purpose is to explain and clarify my own choice of subject, I may perhaps be permitted to speak somewhat dogmatically. Modern philosophy is characteristically *egocentric*. I mean no more than this: that firstly, it takes the Self as its starting-point, and not God, or the world or the community; and that, secondly, the Self is an individual in isolation, an ego or 'I', never a 'thou'. This is shown by the fact that there can arise the question, 'How does the Self know that other selves exist?' Further, the Self so premised is a thinker in search of knowledge. It is conceived as the Subject; the correlate in experience of the object presented for cognition. Philosophy then, as distinct from Science, is concerned with the formal characters of the processes, activities or constructions in and through which the object is theoretically determined. And since the Self is an element, in some sense, of the world presented for knowing, it must be determined through the same forms as every other object.

Now the outstanding feature of the modern development of knowledge has been the creation of the positive sciences, and this has meant that there has been a determining relation between philosophy and science throughout. The relation has not been one-sided, but reciprocal. It has been the task of philosophy to create the conceptual forms and systems of categories which provide the logical structure, and so determine the general attitude of mind favourable to the production and to the reception of scientific knowledge. This was not, on the whole, intentional, except where the philosophical work was carried out by scientists in pursuit of their own objectives; and many philosophers have also been scientists. For the most part the philosophers were concerned to determine general forms of knowledge with a metaphysical or quasi-metaphysical purpose in mind. In particular, they were concerned to determine the formal structure of the Self and its experience, both individual and social, both theoretical and practical, in their character as object for philosophical knowledge.

The result of this interrelation of science and philosophy is that modern philosophy has completed two distinct phases, which correspond respectively to the creation of the physical and of the biological sciences. The first is usually reckoned as running from Descartes to Hume; the second from Kant to the present day. It would be more accurate to see the beginning of the second phase in Rousseau, and its continuation in the German idealist movement from Lessing to Hegel, with Kant standing ambiguously between and stretching out a hand to both. The key-concept of the first phase is 'substance'; its form and method are mathematical. Substance, then, is that which is determined by thought as a mathematical system. Pure mathematics provides the ideal form of all valid knowledge, and whatever cannot be determined in this form is unknowable. Since such indeterminables must in some sense be presented to the self, they must be referred not to the object, but to the subject, and must find their origin in a creative spontaneity of the mind. The process of thought distinguishes between what is objective and what is subjective in experience. The objective is valid: the subjective is unreal, illusory or imaginary.

The crux of the matter comes, for philosophy, in the attempt to determine, in this form, the Self and its activities, and centrally, its activities as thinker. The mathematical form proves adequate for the scientific determination of the material world. But the attempt to conceive the self as substance and to determine it through the mathematical form meets difficulties which prove insuperable, and lead to scepticism. For it becomes clear that the activities of the self in providing the form through which the object is determined themselves involve a constructive spontaneity of the mind—an *a priori* synthesis—for which no objective basis can be assigned; and the substantial self appears to be itself the product of such a subjective construction.

This first phase of modern philosophy arises through a primary attention to the form through which the material world—the world of substantial objects—can be rationally determined. Its problem was the form of the material. It broke down in its effort to universalize this form to cover the whole field of knowledge, and, in particular, in the attempt to conceive the Self on the analogy of the material world. The inadequacy of this analogy lies in the element of spontaneous construction, of self-determining and self-directed development which is present in the activity of the Self, but which is excluded from the conception of the material. The second phase, seeking a more adequate form, turned its attention from the material to the living. For it is in the phenomena of life, and particularly in the processes of growth, that this spontaneity of inner self-determination and directed development seems, at least, to be characteristically manifest. Its key-concept is not substance, but organism, and its problem is the form of the organic. In contrast to the mathematical form, which is a combination of identical units, the organism is conceived as a harmonious balancing of differences, and in its pure form, a tension of opposites; and since the time factor—as growth, development or becoming—is of the essence of life, the full form of the organic is represented as a dynamic equilibrium of functions maintained through a progressive differentiation of elements within the whole.

This proved to provide an adequate conceptual form for the

development of the biological sciences. It is indeed the formal expression of the notion of organic evolution. But as a philosophical conception it is necessarily universal, and is thought as the form of the whole Real. In particular it must be the form of thought, and serve for the conception of the Self and its activities. The Self is no longer a substance, but an organism, and since the Self is still essentially the subject of experience the process of knowledge must appear as a self-determining development in which an original undifferentiated unity differentiates itself progressively while maintaining a functional coherence of its elements. The logical form of thought is no longer mathematical but dialectical; not analytic but synthetic; a progressive synthesis of opposites.

It may be objected that this applies only to the development of Hegelian idealism, and can hardly be said to characterize the philosophy of the last century. There is some truth in this; but it does not touch the major issue, which is not tied to an acceptance, as it stands, of the Hegelian dialectic. It is the dominance of the biological analogy in philosophy which is decisive, and this clearly will cover all organic and evolutionary types of philosophy down to those of Alexander and Whitehead, not to speak of dialectical materialism. But more than this is required to answer the doubt, and I shall offer one or two further suggestions.

The first of these is that the rise of biology did not mean the suppression of physics; correspondingly, the rise of the organic philosophies did not mean the disappearance of the mathematical. The new type of thought developed from the beginning in tension with and under criticism from the older type; but, the older type in its persistence was under the necessity of considering and dealing with the aspects of experience upon which the newer philosophy was concentrating attention, under penalty of ceasing to be contemporary. The second suggestion concerns the development of biology itself. The chemists began to apply the methods of physical science, with their associated system of concepts, in the organic field, and were increasingly successful. The evolutionary hypothesis, though useful and indeed essential up to a point, began to appear as a framework within which the biochemists could build a true *science* of the organic; or even as a scaffolding which would ultimately be dispensed with. In the debate between vitalists and biochemists which followed, it was the biochemists who were victorious. Their success was made possible by, and in turn stimulated, a development of mathematical theory which in the long run amounted to a transformation. The new instruments of mathematical analysis proved capable of representing and elucidating functional and developmental processes and relations.

The corresponding process in philosophy may be briefly summarized. Realism developed as an internal criticism of the organic philosophy, with an empirical temper. The criticism has a double edge. It denies the adequacy of the organic form and its dialectical logic in the philosophical field, as formal analysis of the Self as thinker. This is the realist criticism of the idealist theory of knowledge. It denies also its necessity and its usefulness as an instrument for the empirical analysis of organic process. Until the contemporary break with tradition was established, philosophical realism remained conditioned by and tied to the organic concept, as an antithesis is tied to its thesis. The two aspects of the philosophy are complementary as well as antithetical. If this is concealed from a superficial view it is because of a realist concentration on the positive task of showing that a transformed formal logic based upon the transformation of mathematical theory can provide an instrument of analysis adequate for all scientific purposes. But there is no victory for either party and no synthesis. The development is rather a commentary on the Kantian conclusion that though the teleological idea may have an indispensable heuristic function, all scientific inquiry is necessarily mathematical. But success in this formal task is not self-interpreting. Whitehead and Russell collaborated in *Principia Mathematica*; but while the latter interprets their joint achievement as a refutation of the organic idea, the former interprets it as leading to a realistic philosophy of organism. However firmly realists may reject Hegelianism and its offshoots, and go back behind Kant to link up with the earlier mathematical period, the result is not to reinstate the concept of substance on its throne.

What brings the period to an end is not then the refutation of idealism by the realists, but a relapse into scepticism and the emergence of a new problem. As happens so often in the history of thought, anticipations of this process are to be found. The Danish eccentric, Kierkegaard, discovered that the Hegelian philosophy was ludicrously incapable of solving—even, indeed, of formulating—the problem of 'the existing individual'. If we apply the Hegelian logic to the data of personal reality, we produce, he showed, 'a dialectic without a synthesis'; for the process of the personal life generates a tension of opposites which can be resolved, not by reconciliation but only by a choice between them, and for this choice no rational ground can be discovered. He concluded that we must abandon philosophy for religion, reason for faith. His older contemporary, Auguste Comte, had more in common with him than would at first appear. Both are profoundly under the influence of the organic philosophy; and both are concerned to apply it to the understanding of personal reality. But whereas Kierkegaard emphasizes its individual aspect, Comte is interested in human society. In this, like Karl Marx, he remains closer to Hegel, and to the general philosophical tradition, so that his criticism lacks the depth and the absoluteness of Kierkegaard's. It does not touch the form, but only the content of the organic philosophy. So Comte abandoned metaphysics, that is to say, philosophy as a speculative knowledge of human reality, in favour of science, and therefore of empirical sociology. In the result, he became the founder at once of modern sociology and of modern positivism. Had he been more aware of his own debt to the organic philosophy which he rejected, he would have realized that the *form* of his science of society was of philosophical origin, and his relation to contemporary logical positivism would have been more obvious. He would stand to that aspect of contemporary philosophy as Kierkegaard does to contemporary existentialism; and the relation, in both cases, is highly ambiguous. Kierkegaard would never have admitted that 'existential thinking' could be philosophical; for him it was a form of art. 'I am a poet,' he maintained, 'that is my category.'

There is no reason to suppose that this phase of scepticism is any more final than others that philosophy has overcome in the past. For Comte, as for Kierkegaard, we must remember, philosophy is identified with a particular *type* of philosophy; that type which constructs itself on the form of the organic. If they discover that philosophy is incapable of formulating, either in its individual or its social aspect, the nature of personal experience, this need not mean that philosophy is invalid, but only that an organic conception of the personal is inadequate to the facts. Since philosophy must include the personal in its field of inquiry, this can only mean that we must abandon the organic form as inadequate for the philosophical purpose, and initiate a search for the form of the personal.

If we are correct in suggesting that there is, in the modern period, a close relation between the development of science and of philosophy, this is the conclusion which we shall naturally expect. If science moves from an established physics to the foundation of scientific biology, we find that philosophy moves from a mathematical to an organic form. We should expect, then, that the emergence of a scientific psychology would be paralleled by a transition from an organic to a personal philosophy. The form of the personal will be the emergent problem. Such a new phase of philosophy would rest on the assertion that the Self is neither a substance nor an organism, but a person. Its immediate task would be to discover the logical form through which the unity of the personal can be coherently conceived.

The transition from an organic to a personal conception of unity, however, cannot be so simple as that from a physical to an organic conception. The transformation involved is much more fundamental. The difficulties are of the same type as those which beset the effort to establish psychology on a sure scientific basis. There are two major difficulties. Firstly, so long as psychology is conceived as a science of mind, consciousness or the subjective, it fails. To establish itself it must think of itself as a science of human *behaviour*. Similarly in the philosophical transition, we can no longer conceive the Self as the subject in experience, and so as the knower. The Self must be conceived, not theoretically as subject, but practically, as agent. Secondly, human behaviour is comprehensible only in terms of a dynamic social reference; the isolated, purely individual self is a fiction. In philosophy this means, as we shall see, that the unity of the personal cannot be thought as the form of an individual self, but only through the mutuality of personal relationship. In face of both difficulties a radical modification of our philosophical tradition is demanded. The first requires us to substitute for the Self as subject, which is the starting-point of modern philosophy, the Self as agent; and to make this substitution is to reject the traditional distinction between the subjective and the objective. The second compels us to abandon the traditional individualism or egocentricity of our philosophy. We must introduce the second person as the necessary correlative of the first, and do our thinking not from the standpoint of the 'I' alone, but of the 'you and I'.

This diagnosis of the problem which must be solved and of the two major difficulties in the way of its solution, dictate the procedure which we shall follow. We shall devote ourselves, in this first volume, to a study of the Self as agent, seeking to shift the centre of gravity in philosophical thinking from the theoretical to the practical field. The second volume, under the title *Persons in Relation* will then seek to elucidate the problem of the mutuality of the personal. The full justification of the assertion that these are the two major issues in any effort to determine the form of the personal cannot be offered now. It will, we may hope, reveal itself as we proceed.

CHAPTER TWO

Kant and the Romantics

We have now to determine the nature of our problem more closely, by reference to the history of modern philosophy. For this purpose I shall discuss and criticize, in this and the succeeding chapter, the Critical philosophy of Immanuel Kant. There are two reasons in particular which make this essential. At that point in history, in the first place, as at our own, we find a break with tradition and the emergence of a new problem. In the second place, the Critical philosophy is the most adequate of modern philosophies, and indeed, relatively to all the others, completely adequate; so that in discussing Kant we discuss, in principle, all modern philosophy.

The term 'adequate' is here employed in a somewhat technical sense. The adequacy of a philosophy depends upon its range; upon the extent to which it succeeds in holding together the various aspects of human experience, and exhibiting their unity. Kant is unique in the comprehensive unity of his thought. He does full justice to the first, Cartesian phase of modern philosophy. As to the second, it has been said with truth that all subsequent philosophies have been built out of the ruins of the Critical philosophy. I should prefer to say that until we come to those new tendencies which have been generated by the breakdown of tradition in our own time, every significant movement in philosophy since Kant can be derived from the Critical philosophy by rejecting parts of it; and by reasserting what any of them has rejected, the premisses for its refutation can also be found. Modern philosophies have often gained in coherence by this selectiveness; they have invariably gained this greater consistency at the expense of adequacy.

It was particularly unfortunate that, by the accident of history, objective idealism was the first type of philosophy so to be derived. We have come to regard Kant as the precursor of Hegel. It would be more true to say that the Critical philosophy was written to nip Hegelianism in the bud. The effect of seeing Kant through Hegelian spectacles is to shift the centre of gravity of Kant's thinking so that it falls within the Analytic of the *Critique of Pure Reason*. For Kant himself it falls within the *Critique of Practical Reason*: while the most important section of the first *Critique* is the *Dialectic*. Indeed the vital conclusion of the Critical philosophy as a whole—and it is one which points beyond Kant's own achievement—is that reason is primarily practical.

The immediate background of the Critical philosophy is the Romantic movement. It is a mistake to think of the Romantic movement as a literary and artistic revolution only. It is this, of course; but it is also a revolution in social outlook and in thought. The French revolution was its most volcanic manifestation in the political field. Rousseau was its fountain-head. But in Germany the Romantic movement became the starting-point of an indigenous culture, and a major factor in the creation of the German nation. Here the Romantics became philosophers. Lessing, dramatist and art-critic, produced the first of the philosophies of history in *Religion as the Education of the Human Race*; Herder, the poet, created the idea of Nature as a developing organic system in his *Ideas for a Philosophy of History*. The German romantics combined art and philosophy; they were thinkers as well as men of letters. The result was a process of creative philosophical development which culminated in Hegel. Hegelianism is the mature expression of Romantic philosophy.

The pioneers in this philosophical movement were Lessing, Hamann and Herder. Between them they enunciated the main structural ideas of romantic thought. Lessing contributed the ideas of productive imagination, and of development; Hamann the notion of reality as a tension of contradictions; Herder that of Nature as an organic unity. Of the three it is Hamann who is the most significant for our purpose. He was the founder of the Faith philosophy, with Herder as his younger collaborator. These two were, so far as I know, the first philosophers to appeal to Hume against Kant, reckoning Hume, perhaps not without reason, as a romantic like themselves.[1] In his own day Hamann was an intellectual force of great influence, and was known as the Magus of the North. He had had a revelation, while reading his Bible in Bloomsbury, on a business trip to London. He returned to Königsberg and spent the rest of his life propagating the new idea in the same city as Kant, who knew him well.

The Faith philosophy rests upon a radical opposition between faith and reason. Hamann maintained that reason is an illusory guide to knowledge: we can know reality only by means of faith. The ground for this judgement is that reason works by the law of contradiction, and so uses the absence of contradiction as the guarantee of truth. Faith, on the contrary, reveals reality as a *coincidentia oppositorum*, a tension of contradictory elements. The further the process of reason is carried, therefore, the farther we are from knowledge. Now this antithesis of 'faith' and 'reason' does not carry its meaning on its face, though it marks clearly and unambiguously a complete break with tradition. We need to know to what precisely the terms 'reason' and 'faith' refer. By 'reason' Hamann means all discursive thinking, and in particular Cartesian rationalism and the mathematical methods on which physical science depends. In contrast, faith refers to an inner experience, a living apprehension which carries with it an immediate conviction of its own validity. Terminology is important here, because in the development of the Faith philosophy after Hamann other terms

[1] 'Hume is the man for me for he at least honours the principle of belief, and includes it in his system, while our countryman (sc. Kant) is always chewing the cud of his causal whirligig, without a thought for belief. I don't call that honest.' Hamann in a letter to Herder, 10 May 1781.

were substituted. After Kant's analysis in the first *Critique*, 'reason' was replaced by 'understanding'. 'Faith' proved more difficult, and various expressions were employed as synonyms for it—'inner experience' is one; 'imagination' is another. But in the end, 'faith' is replaced by 'reason', which had lost its function. In the full development of Romantic philosophy, therefore, what began as a contrast between 'faith' and 'reason' appears as a contrast between 'reason' and 'understanding'. In Objective idealism, 'Reason' has come to denote what Hamann had called 'faith' and had contrasted with 'reason'; though in the development its connotation has been enriched.

What is this capacity to grasp reality as a unity of opposites, not discursively but immediately? The proper answer, I believe, is 'aesthetic intuition'. It is the faculty of the mind which Kant calls 'judgement' (*Urteilskraft*) and which forms the subject of the third *Critique*. Significantly, Kant associated it with the apprehension of beauty on the one hand, and on the other with the idea of teleology. We can best define Hamann's contrast of faith and reason by saying that 'reason' is that in us which enables us to produce science; while 'faith' is our capacity for aesthetic experience. Hamann's proposal, whether he is aware of it or not, is to substitute the artist's standpoint for the scientist's, as the basis of our knowledge of the real.

Now this is one of the common themes of romantic literature. 'Beauty is truth', says Keats. Browning is even more explicit, when he makes the organist, Abt Vogler, say,

The rest may reason, and welcome: 'tis we musicians know.

and in the same poem we find a fine metaphorical expression of the dialectical principle linked with it;

*I know not if, save in this, such gift be allowed to man
That out of three sounds he frame, not a fourth sound, but a star.*

That this is also the theme of Romantic philosophy is confirmed by Fichte. Contrasting the standpoints of science and philosophy, he remarks that the standpoint of philosophy is 'counternatural or artistic'.

Against this background the Critical philosophy was written. It is true that Kant was older than any of the thinkers we have referred to. Lessing was five years, Hamann six years younger, Herder twenty. But Kant's thought matured slowly. When the *Critique of Pure Reason* saw the light, Kant was already fifty-seven. His *Inaugural Dissertation* of 1770, eleven years earlier, shows him still in a pre-critical stage. Lessing died before the first *Critique* was published. Hamann came to his philosophical position early. He lived to read and protest against the *Critique of Pure Reason*, but died in 1788, the year in which the second *Critique* came from the press. Even Herder was thirty-seven years of age when the first *Critique* appeared, and though he had been a pupil of Kant's, he joined Hamann in defending the Faith philosophy against Kant, whose mature work they regarded as an attack upon their own position. In spite of Kant's seniority, therefore, all three should be regarded not as successors, but as predecessors of the Critical philosophy.

The question of Kant's relation to the Romantic movement is thus decisive for any understanding of the Critical philosophy. Is Kant in the romantic camp, or is he against it? The answer must be that his attitude is ambiguous. It is an attitude of critical sympathy. For the sympathy the evidence is conclusive. Kant admired Rousseau, and considered the French Revolution, though not its violence, justified. When he described the dialectic of reason as a dialectic of illusion; when he wrote in the Introduction to the second edition of the *Critique of Pure Reason* that 'he found it necessary to deny knowledge in order to make room for faith', is it possible to believe that he had not Hamann in mind? Kant is therefore on the side of the romantics.

But it is a critical sympathy. It may well be that when he called his own doctrine a 'critical idealism' Kant was thinking of the Faith philosophy as an uncritical idealism. The important question is this, 'In what respect was Kant in sympathy with the Romantic philosophy; and wherein was he critical?' A full answer would require a detailed account of Kant's doctrine, and that is clearly out of the question, even if I were competent to give it. We need consider only the relation of the Critical philosophy as a whole, to the emergent problem of its time. The detailed exegesis of the *Critiques* is often controversial, but on its general intent there is little ground for disagreement.

The radical difference between the Romantic philosophy and the philosophy of the Cartesians may best be expressed by reference to the function of the imagination in knowledge. There is a characteristic contrast, commonly drawn in the earlier period, between 'the white light of reason' and 'the colourful fancies of the imagination'. The imagination is the bugbear of rational thought. It cannot be dispensed with altogether, because memory depends upon it. Its task is to reproduce faithfully what has been experienced in the past. But it has a dangerous capacity for playing fast and loose with the material committed to its charge, and producing attractive fancies of its own instead of recording facts. The task of the thinker is to suppress this productive spontaneity and hold the imagination to a purely reproductive function. The Romantics reverse this by insisting that the productive spontaneity of the imagination underlies all experience, and particularly all cognition. This is the radical break with tradition. This is what underlies Hamann's contrast between 'faith' and 'reason'. This is what instigates the substitution of the artistic for the scientific point of view. For the activity of the productive imagination is an artistic activity, and it consists in combining the elements of experience in a way that is not itself given in experience. It is an activity of synthesis. If, as the Faith philosophy asserts, it is the source of knowledge, then all knowledge is synthetic.

Now Kant fully shares this position. He not merely shares it, he establishes it by careful analysis and demonstration. He goes farther in maintaining that our primary perceptual experience itself presupposes a transcendental synthesis, even though at

Kant's critique

first sight it seems to be sheerly 'given'. The root of all knowledge is the productive imagination. It is 'a blind art, hid in the depths of the soul'.

In what then does Kant's criticism of the Faith philosophy consist? Simply in this; that while the other Romantics were cheering madly because they had discovered the solution to the problem of knowledge, Kant realized that they had made the problem a hundred times more difficult than it had been before. The discovery that the productive synthesis of the imagination is the root of all knowledge makes knowledge itself problematical. For it means that we invent our knowledge; that knowledge, in some sense, is fictional. If this is so, how can it be knowledge? For knowledge is the discovery of what is already there; it is factual not fictional, a receptivity and not a spontaneity of the mind. If the knower is the imaginative artist, how are we to distinguish between fact and fiction? Thus the new discovery, which he accepts, becomes for Kant the new problem for philosophy. Characteristically he generalizes it, concentrates upon its purely formal and universal aspect, and formulates it as the problem of the Critical philosophy, 'How are synthetic judgements *a priori* possible?'

Instead of attempting to summarize Kant's abstract argument, I shall risk the raising of eyebrows among the pundits and offer a concrete interpretation of its meaning so far as it concerns us here. If we take the new discovery at its face value, without criticism, as the romantics do, what must happen? We shall subsume all aspects of our experience under the form of aesthetic activity. In particular we shall develop an aesthetic science and an aesthetic morality. Both theoretical and practical experience will be determined by artistic standards. Both the good and the true will become 'that which satisfies the mind', the one in the practical, the other in the theoretical field. This can only result in the destruction both of science and of morality. What satisfies the mind is the beautiful. The good, however, is what we *ought* to do, whether we like it or not. The true is what we *ought* to believe, however much it goes against our inclinations. If then all experience is shown to rest on the blind art of an imaginative synthesis the problem it sets philosophy is to distinguish science and morality from art; and indeed to distinguish also the mere play of fancy from art as a serious and deliberate activity of mature human beings. For this reason Kant had to write three *Critiques*, the first about science, the second about morality and the third about art; and throughout he was concerned to defend rationality against the romantic attack. If he had to deny knowledge, he would not, with Hamann, repudiate reason.

Let us begin with the denial of knowledge. Knowledge is, in some sense, the discovery of what exists independently of any activity of ours. If we construct our knowledge, if it depends at all upon a spontaneous, inventive activity of the mind, then there is no escape from the conclusion that we can never know the world as it is in itself, independently of our ways of apprehending it. A sheerly passive receptivity, in which Reality should impress itself upon the blankness of our ignorance, is completely ruled out. Reality as it is in itself is unknowable. This is the famous doctrine of the Thing-in-itself, of the noumenal world, and it is Kant's denial of knowledge. The discovery of a law of nature by science is the construction of a mathematical formula, and mathematical formulae are human inventions. So far Hamann was right in his attack upon discursive thought.

What Hamann failed to notice, however, is that this applies equally to what he called 'faith'. Aesthetic intuition, for all its immediacy, is a synthetic activity. Suppose we rule out thought altogether, what remains? A pure immediacy of sense perception, in which a world of objects is revealed to us? Not at all. The artist, who really does try to see the world with an innocent eye, discovers simply a pattern of coloured shapes, which changes as we watch it; or a pattern of sounds, in which a theme repeats itself with variations. For pure intuition there are no 'objects'; these have to be discriminated against a background. When we become as little children, who have not yet learned to discriminate, objects fade into their background and leave only a pattern of differences in space and time.

At this level of pure intuition, however, the distinction between perception and imagination has disappeared. What we see with closed or open eyes is the same thing—a spatio-temporal pattern of coloured shapes. And the space and time which holds the elements together is the same space and the same time in both cases. When we shut our eyes and imagine a scene, what we see is a pattern in space and time. When we open them different colours and shapes take their place in the same space and time. So space and time are the forms, not of our perception, but of our intuition, whether perceptual or imaginary. How then do we come to perceive, not a pattern of sense-data, but a world of objects? The answer must be that we do this by a further activity of discriminating, within the pattern, certain groups of elements which we isolate and hold together against the rest of the pattern as a background. We now do this automatically, by recognizing objects which we have often discriminated in the past; but once upon a time, in our infancy, we had to learn to do it. At the other end of the scale, the scientist returns, as it were, to the original pattern and discriminates it afresh, in different groupings of its elements, to produce a picture of the world very different from the one that our ordinary perceptual discrimination offers us.

We must confine ourselves, however, to those general features of Kant's doctrine which are essential to our particular purpose. The major point, which applies both to the theoretical and to the practical problem, both to science and to morality, is this. The pattern which underlies all aspects of our experience depends upon our sensuous equipment. Its elements are our sense-data. But it is a pattern; it has a structure which unifies it; and that structure is spatio-temporal. That structure too, is ours. It is the form of our imagination, common to the world of fancy and of fact. So it follows that if we know the world at all, it is the world as it appears to us, taking upon it the forms of our mode of intuition, and not the world as it is in its independent being. How then can our imaginative construction ever be true or false? How can our actions ever be right or wrong? How can we ever get beyond a synthesis that satisfies us?

Kant answers by reference to law. There are two types of law which we recognize—the law of Nature and the moral law. The first prescribes how things must happen: it is descriptive. The second is normative, and prescribes how things ought to happen. The synthesis of art is a free synthesis; we can combine the elements of intuition—sounds and colours—as we please, to satisfy ourselves. But when we think in order to discover the truth, or when we act with a view to doing what is right, the synthesis is not free; it must conform to a law which dictates its form. We can indeed think what pleases us, we can do what satisfies our inclination; but so neither knowledge nor morality is possible. They become possible through conformity to a rule.

Consider knowledge first. How is the spatio-temporal pattern transformed in perception into a world of objects? By combining elements selected from the pattern in the right way. What is the right way? The way that does transform the pattern into a world of objects. This doesn't seem to mean anything; it appears to be simply ringing the changes. But is it? When I say that one and one make two I enunciate a rule for counting. If you ask why I shouldn't say one and one make three, the answer is that you can say what you please; but if you want to count that is the rule, and if you don't count in that way then you just aren't counting. There is only one way to count things. In that case the rule both prescribes the method of counting and describes the process of counting. So in thinking. You can think as you please, of course; but if you are trying to get at the truth then there is only one way to think. Any other way is not really thinking. So thought is an activity which conforms to a law—or a system of laws which is one law—and we can call the law either **a** rule which prescribes how we are to think or a description of the process of thinking. It is at once the rule for thinking and the form of thought.

KANT AND THE ROMANTICS

Knowledge, says Kant, is the determination of an object by means of concepts. To determine an object, we can see, is to combine the elements of the sensuous pattern—or rather a selection of them—so as to constitute an object; or, more generally, to break up and recombine the elements so that we perceive a world of objects. But what is a concept? It is a rule for doing this. The concept of a triangle, says Kant, is a rule for the construction of any triangle. It is equally the form of a triangle, the means by which we recognize a triangle when we see it. Now the process of determining an object is a process of understanding; it is a process of making sense of the meaningless pattern of sense-data. If it seems that Kant is making mountains out of molehills one should ask this question. What is there that is common to a coloured shape and a sound that could link them together when we see a blackbird on the apple-tree and hear it singing? Surely nothing at all. Sound and colour are sheerly different. If they are to be combined there must be a rule for their combination if any object is to emerge. The rules are concepts; concepts belong to the understanding; and the principle of understanding which makes knowledge possible is that there is only one way in which we can make sense of our experience; that is to say, determine it by thought as a single world of objects in systematic relation with one another.

The concepts of the understanding are either pure or empirical. Empirical concepts are derived from experience. They are the forms of things—that is, combinations of sense-data—which we have learned to distinguish and which recur again and again. As rules, they are rules for recognizing new instances of a type with which we are already familiar. Because they are formed in this way, there is always a possibility of error in their use. I may perceive a rabbit in a field on a country walk, and it may turn out as I come nearer to be the stump of a tree. I saw an object, and misjudged it by subsuming the sense-data under the wrong empirical concept. Consequently all empirical determinations of things require verification by reference to further experience. But these empirical determinations are possible only because there are pure concepts which are not produced in this way, but are completely general, and presupposed in all experience. For example, there is nothing in the spatio-temporal pattern in intuition to suggest that its elements should be grouped into objects. This implies that if we do discover objects in it, we must already possess the idea of an object, as a universal form, or a universal rule for determining any object whatever. These pure concepts Kant calls the categories of the understanding.

The categories themselves form a compact system. Each implies the others and there is no place for any extra. Together they constitute the law to which thought must conform; or—for it is the same thing—the form of the process of thinking. Thinking again, is the process of imaginative synthesis in so far as it conforms to the rule. It organizes the data of intuition in the form dictated by the categories. Now the data of intuition have their own form, which is spatio-temporal. So when thought determines objects, the form of thought combines with the spatio-temporal form of intuition to produce a schema, or a schematic system, and this schematic system is the form of the world which we perceive. When the productive imagination, conforming to the rules of the understanding, generates this spatio-temporal schematism, it provides a form which is both the form of our knowing and the form of the world we know. This is why Kant says that the understanding gives laws, not merely to our search for knowledge, but to Nature. For the structure of thought and the structure of Nature are necessarily identical.

This brings us to the supreme principle of knowledge, which Kant, echoing Descartes, calls the 'Cogito', the 'I think' which accompanies all my representations; or, in his technical terminology, the transcendental unity of apperception. If we abstract from thought, what remains is the spatio-temporal pattern of sense data, which Kant calls the manifold in intuition. Here, as we saw, there is no distinction between imagining and perceiving. Every element in the pattern is an intuition of mine.

It is this reference to one and the same centre of experience, which gives the data their primary unity as elements in our experience. They are all mine. But when we drop the abstraction, this experiencing centre (the 'I') becomes the thinking Self—not the 'I' but the 'I think'. To think is to determine an object; so the fact that the manifold in intuition stands under the unity of thought transforms it into a world of objects, in systematic relation with one another in space and time. The form of thought which the pattern takes on is the form of a world that is comprehensible to us. The elements of the pattern which were simply 'my sensations' are referred to the object, as my representation of it. The red which I sense becomes the colour of a rose; the sound I hear becomes a blackbird's song. Intuition is discriminated into imagination and perception. So I perceive the world, and distinguish between the world and myself. I am the Subject; the world is the Object. My imaginings are subjective; but what I think is objective. This dichotomy of Subject and Object is the abstract form of all our knowledge. Subject and Object are correlatives, or polar opposites which depend upon one another, and the principle of their correlation is that the form of thought is the form of the object. For this reason Kant insisted that the transcendental unity of apperception is an objective unity. To know is to apprehend an object. Truth is objectivity.

If we ask at this point whether Kant has solved the problem of distinguishing between art and science, by showing how knowledge can be at once an invention of the mind and a discovery of the truth, the answer is ambiguous. In a sense he has. He has distinguished clearly between an imaginative synthesis that is fanciful, that satisfies us, and a synthesis that is necessary and which we are under an obligation to make and to accept. The antithesis of faith and reason in Hamann's philosophy, which substitutes the inner conviction of the truth of an imaginative synthesis for discursive thought as the source of knowledge, has been completely exploded. On the other hand the new idea which it embodies has been accepted and restated, as the result of a more highly developed analysis. For lack of this analysis Hamann had drawn hasty and unwarrantable conclusions. But knowledge is still synthetic, and the constructive activity of imagination remains its basis. Though it needs thought to discriminate and verification to confirm it, the world is still dependent on the mind for its very existence. I construct the world I know, even if I construct it in accordance with the laws of thought.

Yes, but this is ambiguous. As a particular individual I am only one object in the world which is determined by thought. My thinking itself, as a process that takes place in my mind, is part of the process of events in the world. The world that I know contains me as a part of it, determined by the categories, and if I exist then in the same sense the world exists, outside me, and totally independent of me as a particular individual. That there is only one way to count does not mean that I cannot miscalculate; and my private thinking may lead me into error. My errors of judgement make no difference to the structure of the world. The objective unity of the 'I think' is not the unity of any particular experience. It is the unity of all possible experience; the logical correlate of the one existing world of objects.

Why then should not the Faith philosophy take up all this into itself and so reach a higher stage of its own development? There is only one reason; it is Kant's insistence that there is a real world, unknowable by us, of which the world constructed by thought is only the appearance. We know only phenomena. Of the real world of things-in-themselves we can only say that we know that it exists; but we cannot know at all what it is. It remains for ever undeterminable by thought. As is well known, the mature development of the romantic philosophy, in Fichte, Schelling and Hegel depended upon accepting in principle Kant's analysis and rejecting the doctrine of the two worlds. In this way the world we know becomes again the real world, as it was for Hamann. More important still, knowledge remains, though at a higher level, fundamentally aesthetic. For truth becomes simply the comprehensive coherence of the imaginative synthesis.

It must be admitted that the doctrine of things-in-themselves is objectionable; and that if it goes then Kant's theory of knowledge can easily be transformed—as in fact it was—into a dialectical idealism like Hegel's. The result is a more coherent philosophy; but also a much less adequate one. For what we have considered of the Critical philosophy is only the first two parts of the first *Critique*. So far there is no good ground for believing in the existence of a noumenal world. The reason for the doctrine of things-in-themselves is foreshadowed in the final section of the first *Critique*, but only becomes fully apparent in the *Critique of Practical Reason*, the function of which is to distinguish morality from art, and so to defeat the romantic tendency to produce an aesthetic determination of the good.

In the Dialectic of the *Critique of Pure Reason* Kant for the first time comes to grips with reason itself. It is the understanding which is concerned with the knowledge we have of the world of objects. The understanding does its work by applying the categories to the manifold of intuition. Reason must be distinguished from understanding. It has its 'ideas' which are concerned with the ultimate nature of things, with the unconditioned; while the understanding determines objects by discovery of their conditions. We are therefore tempted to use the ideas of reason, which are pure formal concepts, to provide knowledge of what lies beyond the conditioned existence of the world we know in sensuous experience. There arises in this way a dialectic of reason, and the product of this dialectic is metaphysics. What then is the place of reason in knowledge? Kant's answer is twofold. First, the dialectic of reason is a dialectic of illusion. All metaphysics, that is, all knowledge of the supersensuous, is nonsense. We can know only by determining the structure of a world given in sense perception. The moment we speculate about what cannot be given perceptually, we can produce theories in plenty, but since they have content, and are not merely formal, they require verification; and they cannot be verified. Here Kant reveals himself as a positivist. Secondly, the ideas of reason, being concepts, are rules or principles which guide the understanding in the production of knowledge. Thus reason is a higher principle than understanding. It is not itself a faculty of cognition, but it provides the understanding with the practical rules for the use of the categories in the search for knowledge. So as regards reason, provided again that we distinguish it from understanding, Hamann is right. The use of pure reason to give us knowledge of reality is the source of illusion.

It is only when we turn to consider our practical experience as agents, and not our theoretical experience as thinkers, that we discover the true character of reason. This is the final and quite revolutionary conclusion of the Critical philosophy. Reason is primarily practical. It is not a faculty of cognition, but a faculty of rules. If it has a secondary, theoretical function that is because thinking is something that we do; so that Reason is necessary to provide the rules that guide our search for knowledge. The understanding, which is theoretical, is, as it were, the viceroy of reason in the theoretical field. Reason itself is the ultimate legislator. This is the dignity of reason. For Kant—and as a philosopher—action is more important than knowledge. If it was important to distinguish science from art, it is much more important to distinguish morality from art. The major danger which Kant saw in the uncritical idealism of the romantics was this confusion—the danger of substituting aesthetic for moral standards in the determination of conduct. Indeed science itself, as a human activity, depends upon practical rationality.

The problem of action is set by the antinomy of freedom and determinism. Morality presupposes freedom. Science presupposes determinism. Knowledge is the determination of an object, but this determination is theoretical. If the object can be determined by thought, by a judgement which may be true or false, then it must already be determinate. If it were not determinate, no judgement of ours could be either false or true.

Action, however, is the determination of something not in theory, but in actual fact. To act is to make something other than it would have been if we had not determined it. In knowing an object we make no difference to it: in acting upon it we do make a difference to *it*. Now our actions, as events in the world we know, must be as completely determined as everything else. But in action we presuppose that we determine the world by our actions. The correlative of this freedom is that the world which we determine in action must be indeterminate, capable of being given a structure that it does not already possess. We can only know a determinate world; we can only act in an indeterminate world. Therefore, if we really do act, if our freedom of will is not an illusion, the world in which we act must be unknowable.

This is the fundamental ground of Kant's belief that there must be a real world, behind the phenomenal world, which we cannot know. If there is not, it becomes impossible to distinguish between an aesthetic and a moral praxis. An aesthetic praxis would consist in determining a future state of affairs—an ideal —as the good, and therefore as the end to which our actions ought to be the means. If we could do this, then all we should need to enable us to act rightly would be the scientific under-standing of the causal process which would connect the present state of affairs with the future state which is the good. We could plan our Utopia. Why not? *Because the determination of the good as an object in time is necessarily aesthetic;* it rests upon an inner con-viction which cannot be verified. Conceptual thought could at most tell us that such a state of affairs is possible, and how we can realize it—but not that it is the good. If we are none the less convinced that it is, this can only mean that we have presented to our minds an imaginative synthesis which we feel to be fully satisfactory. The hall-mark of the aesthetic stand-point is that it defines both the true and the good as 'that which satisfies the mind'. This is the proper definition of the beautiful, and the satisfaction is a disinterested satisfaction. But if we confuse this with the morally good, then our Utopia takes on the character of a moral determination. It becomes universally obligatory as the objective of action. Suppose then that there is a person who finds himself possessed of such a vision of the good, convinced by an inner sense of felt and disinterested necessity; suppose that he happens also to possess the power to compel other men to co-operate with him in realizing this good—then it becomes not merely right, but a moral duty for him so to compel them. Their refusal to accept the objective must be judged to be immoral. Being wise after the event, we can say that Kant was warning the German people that if they accepted the romantic philosophy, they would find themselves in the end, with their freedom lost, under the fanatical dictatorship of an Adolf Hitler. There is an interesting statement in Kant's *Lectures on Ethics*, which even if it is precritical is worth a reference. He has been saying things with which we are familiar in the *Fundamental Principles of the Metaphysics of Ethics*; and he suddenly breaks off and warns his students against the dangers of a purely formal ethic. 'God wants men to be made happy by men,' he exclaims, 'and if only all men united to promote their own happiness, we could make a paradise of Nova Zembla.'[1]

If the good, then, cannot be a determinate object at which we aim, if it is theoretically unknowable, there is no way in which we can determine the rule of right action as the means to the good. However far science may advance, knowledge brings us no nearer to an empirical determination of what we ought to do. We can determine rules of prudence through knowledge, and improve them as our knowledge improves. But even if they were certain, as they never can be, they would only determine the means to satisfy our inclinations, and these of course vary from one man to another, and from time to time. The rules of moral action must be rules for achieving an end which we cannot theoretically determine. How is this possible? Only by acting in conformity to a law which is determined for us by reason. The primary function of reason, as legislator, is to prescribe the moral law, which must then be a law which is

[1] I. Kant, *Lectures on Ethics* (trans. L. Infield), p. 55.

universally and absolutely binding on all rational beings, and also a law which of necessity we cannot understand. For to understand it we should have to determine the good as an object in time—as a future Utopia, as the end of the process of Nature. To do this would be to substitute an aesthetic for a moral determination.

We said that all this must follow unless our belief in freedom is an illusion; and this, as we see, means unless there is a world in which our actions determine the good, without our knowledge. But how do we know that we are free agents? Kant's reply is that we do not and cannot. In the moral field we are beyond the limits of knowledge. Then why should freedom not be illusory, and determinism the truth? Kant answers that we *must* believe in freedom. We are in the field of faith, where only belief is possible. But beliefs, like judgements, are not all on the same level. There are necessary beliefs; there are beliefs which though not strictly necessary, are yet reasonable beliefs; and there are beliefs which are not even reasonable, but merely fanciful. The belief in freedom is necessary, in the strictest sense. It is a necessity of reason, like the belief in the law of contradiction. To reject it is to reject reason itself, not merely in the practical, but also in the theoretical field. For we have already seen that the understanding, with its presupposition of total determination in the world, rests upon the law of reason. Indirectly, therefore, the belief that our judgements can be true or false, depends upon our belief that our actions can be right or wrong, of which indeed it is a special case. To believe something because it is true, and not because we want to believe it, is to act, in the field of theory, from duty and not from inclination. Reason is *primarily* practical.

On the rational necessity of a belief in freedom Kant grounds two other beliefs, which though not in the same sense necessary, are yet, he holds, eminently reasonable. They are the beliefs in God and in immortality. Rules of action are rules for the realization of an end. If then we are bound by the laws of reason to act morally, it is reasonable to believe that the course of action so dictated is the means to the realization of the good, even though we cannot determine what the good is. Also there is no determinable relation between the ends which we realize in this world by doing our duty and the good. The good, in realization, is happiness. There is no determinate relation, in experience, between duty and happiness. It is reasonable therefore to believe in a future life in which the good is actually realized as the end to which moral action is the means. And since the union of duty and happiness—as means and end—must be a practical synthesis, it is reasonable to believe in a supreme Agent who achieves this synthesis in practice.

Having distinguished science and morality from the mere synthesis of the productive imagination, through the idea of law; having established reason as the lawgiver, and grounded the theoretical in the practical law of reason; Kant turns, in the third *Critique*, to the field of art. For there is clearly a distinction to be drawn between the blind art which underlies all experience, and the deliberate artistry which is one of the modes of human activity, with a principle of discrimination of its own. In the decade that had elapsed since the publication of the first *Critique*, the development of the Faith philosophy had gone ahead. Herder, in particular, was applying its principle to Nature, and the result was the conception of Nature as an organic system developing itself progressively in history. A new science of Nature, based upon aesthetic intuition, which claimed to supersede mathematical physics was now not merely proposed. It was in active prosecution. A *Critique of (Aesthetic) Judgement* was a necessary completion to the Critical Philosophy.

The third *Critique* is no more a philosophy of art than the second is a moral philosophy. Its purpose is to analyse the discrimination of the beautiful, and so to distinguish it from the discrimination of the true. To emphasize this we might reasonably formulate the question as follows: 'What is it that inclines us to attribute truth to the artistic synthesis, and even a superior truth; and is there any justification at all for this tendency?'

We can summarize Kant's answer in a few sentences for our present purpose. Here, without question, we are dealing with imaginative synthesis in intuition. But we discriminate among such syntheses by judging that some are beautiful and some are not. Now this judgment is not grounded in a concept; it is not therefore an understanding of the object, and consequently it is not knowledge. The ground of our judgement is a feeling of satisfaction which refers to the form of what is apprehended. But the pleasure we find in contemplating the beautiful is not the satisfaction of a particular need or interest of ours. It is a disinterested satisfaction. It appeals to us, not as particular individuals, but as cognitive beings. It satisfies the mind. Because of this our judgement claims to be universally valid, and not a matter of private taste. This can only mean that the form of the synthesis is adapted to our mode of apprehension, through the interrelation of intuition and conception. It fulfils the conditions for our cognition perfectly, and is therefore an ideal object. But it is not cognized; for if it were, it would be in accordance with a rule, and the validity of our judgement could be demonstrated or verified by reference to experience. This explains our tendency to treat the immediate inner conviction that the beautiful occasions in us as a guarantee of truth. It also reveals the illusory character of this conviction. The fatal error is the assumption that truth is what satisfies the mind. Truth is what is determined in accordance with a law, and can be guaranteed only by reference to the law.

This does not, however, mean that aesthetic judgement has no function at all in relation to knowledge. Provided that we do not confuse art with science by confusing the judgement of beauty with the judgement of truth, as the Romantics do, we may find it not merely useful but even necessary to the progress of knowledge. It is clear—though this is not the important point —that the formation of a scientific hypothesis, apart from its verification, is analagous to the production of an artistic synthesis. But the essential issue is the relation of the judgement of beauty to the teleological idea; for the critique of teleological judgement is Kant's mature criticism of all romantic thought, of which Hegelianism is the full flowering.

In analysing the teleological idea, Kant has in mind any attempt to attribute purposiveness to Nature. This is the root concept of any attempt to produce a philosophy of history, like Lessing's or Herder's, or to represent Nature as a developing organic unity, as Herder was doing. In exhibiting the intimate relation of teleology with beauty, Kant was recognizing the essentially artistic standpoint of the Faith philosophy. In recognizing beauty we are recognizing a form of imaginative synthesis which is adapted to the satisfaction of our minds. It is as if the object had been constructed in order to give us a disinterested pleasure in its contemplation. In the case of a work of art this is actually so. In the case of natural beauty it seems to be so. We think of Nature as an artist painting the rose and composing the blackbird's song for our delight. The adaptation, though it may be *to* our minds, is *in* the object. It lies in the inner relations of its parts, in the harmony and balance of their organization, so that each part has a function in the felt unity of the whole.

Now if we seek to know Nature in this way, we must conceive her as a work of art, and therefore as an organic unity, in which every part is functionally related to all the others, and the whole is the embodiment of a developing purpose. But what would this purpose be? Only the production of an ideal object for our satisfaction as cognitive beings. We can only view Nature in this way by taking ourselves as the end to which creation strives. Such a purpose is wholly subjective. We are objectifying it illicitly by projecting our purpose of knowing Nature upon the world, and representing it as Nature's purpose to be known by us. No doubt we shall find ways of concealing the glaring subjectivity and egoism from ourselves in mystical language. We may talk of 'Nature' or 'Reality' or 'the Absolute' knowing itself in us. But such language is only the regular subterfuge of transcendental metaphysics.

Nevertheless there is a necessary part to be played in knowledge by the teleological idea. Its function, says Kant, is heuristic, and it provides a regulative principle in the search for a true knowledge of Nature. A blind investigation will be fruitless. We must bring with us an ideal—a formal notion of what would satisfy our minds if we could find it. Even in mathematical sciences we must assume that Nature is governed by a system of empirical law which is adapted to our modes of knowing. We cannot know in advance that this is so; and we may find, as science progresses, that the complexities of empirical structure are beyond our powers. Again, the idea of Nature as an organic whole is illusory, since it involves the thought that Nature is a finite totality, when in fact it is infinite. Time does not end with us, and we have no ground for assuming that time must have a stop. Yet within nature we do find totalities which arrest our attention with this immediate conviction of purposive, functional unity. Plants and animals are only the most obvious examples. Nature does seem to produce objects which are adapted to our modes of cognition and to display a purposiveness in their organization, even if it is a purposiveness without a purpose. In such cases Nature seems to designate objects appropriate to our search for knowledge. But the satisfaction our minds find in their discovery is not itself knowledge. It selects an object to be known. To know it we must accept it as a whole, within Nature, and analyse its construction. That analysis and the knowledge to which it leads are necessarily mathematical. Even a science of biology must, therefore, be a biophysics.

So Kant defines, critically and negatively, his relation to the Romantics. We might sum up his final argument in contemporary language quite simply. All knowledge of Nature is empirical; and all empirical knowledge must be verifiable. If it is not verifiable it is illusory. What is characteristic of the artist's productions, and of artistic experience as a whole is that it does not and cannot verify its synthesis. The poet may anticipate the scientist; but even if his insight prove true, it is not thereby scientific. It is at best the suggestion of a hypothesis which science may, in its own systematic development, find verifiable.

CHAPTER THREE

The Rejection of Dualism

I was concerned in the last chapter to offer a comment on the Critical philosophy for several reasons. I wished to show how a great philosoper of the past dealt with the emergent problem of a revolutionary epoch. I wanted, also, to exhibit the adequacy of Kant's philosophy as a whole. By this adequacy I intend two closely related characters; firstly, that against the romantic tendency to subsume science and morality under the artistic standpoint, so creating a philosophy of organic development, Kant insisted on distinguishing the three types of judgement on which science, morality and art respectively depend, while at the same time exhibiting their systematic relation; secondly, that the Critical philosophy contains the possibility of all the major types of philosophy which modern Europe has produced from Descartes to the present time, with the possible exception of those which are the emergent philosophies of our own revolution. Both the rationalist and the realist tendencies of the Cartesian period are taken up into the Critical philosophy and their fundamental purpose is defended against the romantic attack. As for subsequent philosophies, they can be derived from Kant by a suitable suppression of recalcitrant doctrines. Objective idealism was derived from the Critical philosophy by suppression of the thing-in-itself. Modern realism, whether organic or mathematical in type, can be similarly derived, as can positivism. These later types of thought, though often more coherent within their limits, are much less adequate; and the basis for their criticism can also be found in Kant. Their inadequacy lies in this, that they fail to hold together, as the Critical philosophy does, the different aspects of human experience. They are, in fact, mainly concerned with knowledge and indeed with scientific knowledge only; and fail to give such an account of science as will be compatible with an aesthetic and a moral philosophy. They fail, to use Kant's language, to deny knowledge in order to make room for faith.

This adequacy of Kant's work is made possible, as he himself insists, by the doctrine of the 'Thing-in-itself'. Suppress this doctrine of the unknowable reality, and the Critical philosophy comes to pieces at the joints. For it is this alone that enables Kant to do justice both to science and to morality. The failure of subsequent thought to reach beyond the boundaries of the foundation laid by Kant is a failure to find any more satisfactory theory to perform this function. There is reason, therefore, to hope that we may find in the Critical philosophy, as a result of its adequacy, the suggestion that we need to carry us beyond it: and it is likely to lie in the central and revolutionary conclusion that reason is primarily not cognitive, but practical.

We must now turn to the criticism of Kant's philosophy as a whole; leaving aside all questions of detail, however important. There are two major criticisms to be made, one concerning its coherence, the other with reference to its adequacy. The first is that there is a radical incoherence in Kant's method of relating the theoretical and the practical activities of Reason: the second that he fails to do justice to the religious aspect of human experience.

The incoherence of the Critical philosophy centres in the doctrine of the thing-in-itself. The function of this doctrine is to resolve the antinomy of freedom; the criticism, that it fails to perform this function satisfactorily. Kant's programme was to distinguish the objective validity of scientific and of moral judgement from the subjective validity of aesthetic judgement. He does this by reference to law—in the one case to natural law, in the other to moral law. Now these two types of law are antithetical. The first is a law of determinism; the second a law of freedom. If there is to be a rational knowledge, the object of knowledge must be already determinate. The determination of the object by a theoretical judgement must, if it is to be true, be a discovery, not merely an invention. On the other hand, if there is to be rational action, then the object of action—what is acted upon—must be indeterminate. For to act is to determine, not a representation of the object, but the object itself. This indeed is what Kant expresses in his definition of the Will as 'a kind of causality belonging to living beings so far as they are rational'.[1] The same world clearly cannot both be completely determined and, even partially, indeterminate. This is the antinomy. Kant resolves it by distinguishing two worlds—the world of things as they appear to us and the world of things as they are in themselves. The former, the phenomenal world, is completely determinate, and therefore knowable; and its determinateness arises from its spatio-temporal character. The latter, the noumenal world, is not spatio-temporal—space and time being forms of our intuition—and is therefore not subject to the determination which knowledge presupposes. But for that very reason it is necessarily unknowable. Both these worlds are independent of us as particular persons, and we are members of both. On the other hand, they cannot be independent of one another, for then our noumenal being and our phenomenal being would be totally unrelated, and we could neither think both nor act in both. In some sense, therefore, the two worlds must be one world. We can think their unity only by taking the noumenal world as the real world, and the phenomenal as its appearance to us in the guise that our spatio-temporal form of intuition imposes upon it. Such language is necessarily analogical, for the relation between the known and the unknowable cannot be formulated otherwise. The analogy is drawn from perceptual experience, where we need at times to distinguish between what something appears to be and what it really is.

[1] Kant, *Fund. Princ. of Metaphys. of Ethics*, trans. Abbott, Third Section (p. 78).

THE REJECTION OF DUALISM

The question, then, is whether this distinction between the noumenal and the phenomenal does provide a solution for the antinomy of freedom. Consider how Kant uses it to solve the problem of the moral struggle, which he rightly sees to be the crux of the matter. There exists in us a tension between inclination and duty. This tension implies that we are capable of action in two modes, from inclination or from duty. In the former mode we act for the satisfaction of our desires, in the latter in conformity to the law of practical reason. In acting from inclination I act as a member of the phenomenal world, since I determine empirically what my desire is and what would satisfy it, and so can calculate the means to a determinate end. In the latter I act as a member of the noumenal world, by conforming to a rule of reason. In this mode I cannot determine an end to which my action should be the means. But my inclinations are themselves phenomenal, and so themselves determined. When therefore I act from inclination my action is determined. When I act in conformity to the moral law, then I act freely.

Now it needs no great argument to show that this distinction of phenomenal and noumenal worlds fails of its purpose. If I am free to act either in the one world—as phenomenon—or in the other—as noumenon—I cannot be a member of either but must have my being beyond both. In that case the distinction of the two worlds fails to account for the struggle in myself. If, on the other hand, I am a member of both, it cannot be in the same sense. For the two worlds differ in status; one is the real world, the other a world of appearances. In that case the moral struggle is not explained, but explained away. For there can be no real struggle between the real and its appearance. We should only be entitled to say that all our actions are really free though they necessarily appear to us to be determined. There is no way that I can find out of this dilemma. It does not help to take Kant's meaning to be that our acts are determined though our wills are free. Will is the conception of the self as agent, and a will which determined nothing but itself would be an illusory will, a cause which was without effect. Here then is the central incoherence of the Critical philosophy. If the moral struggle is to be real, the opponents, sensibility and the rational will, must be *equally* real. If one belongs to the world of appearance and the other to the world of reality then the contest is between a man and his shadow. There is a formal impossibility that the rational will should be overcome, or even influenced by sensibility, if sensibility is phenomenal. For this would mean that the world of appearance could determine the world of reality.

It is important to realize that this is a *formal* inconsistency. It arises through Kant's determination to do full justice to the facts both of scientific and of moral experience, and so to achieve a philosophical adequacy. Formally, it means that the doctrine of the thing-in-itself must be given up. For the justification of this conception lies in the claim that it enables us to think the unity of the same self in the theoretical and the practical fields. If it does not do this—as it does not—then there is no ground for retaining it. But if we reject the doctrine, we must be aware of the consequences. The 'Thing-in-itself' is no excrescence upon the critical teaching: it is not a hang-over from a pre-critical phase of Kant's thinking. Without it the theoretical and the practical aspects of our experience lose relation and fall apart. If Kant's solution fails, then another solution must be found if philosophical adequacy is to be achieved. For it is essential to philosophy that a means should be discovered of thinking coherently the unity of experience as a whole.

The common objection that experience cannot be a totality and so cannot be thought as a unity is beside the point, and Kant himself would surely have treated it with contempt. For no philosopher has ever insisted with greater force that the world we know cannot be a totality; yet none has ever made a more strenuous effort to achieve systematic adequacy in philosophy by thinking the unity of experience. The unity of experience as a whole is not a unity of knowledge, but a unity of personal activities of which knowledge is only one. It consists in the fact that the same person may be at once scientist, artist, moral agent and sinner. We must therefore consider whether this particular expression of formal incoherence—the failure of the doctrine of the 'Thing-in-itself'—is not the consequence of a more general and equally formal inconsistency.

The incoherence arises in the attempt to relate theory and practice. Now the formal principle upon which the whole critical exposition rests is the 'I think'—the transcendental unity of apperception. This signifies that Kant constructs his philosophy on the presupposition that the theoretical is primary. That this is the case is shown, not merely by an analysis of the structure of the Critical philosophy, but by the fact that the problem he bequeathed to his successors is a problem of knowledge, even in the field of morality. Even for the moralists who stand closest to Kant, the ethical problem is theoretical; for it takes the form expressed in the question, 'How can we discriminate between truth and falsity in ethical judgements?' Yet the central conclusion of the Critical philosophy is that reason is primarily practical. To the question, 'How can I know that what I do is right?' Kant's answer, strictly expressed, is that I cannot, since the objective of moral action is indeterminable. At most I can know how to act rightly. By implication, something similar must be said in the theoretical field. To the question, 'How can I know what I should think?' the proper critical answer must be, 'You cannot; what you can know is how to think rightly, in conformity with the rules which reason lays down for the employment of the understanding'. Yet even Fichte, who thought to start from the primacy of the practical, failed to maintain it, and subordinated the practical to the theoretical. For though he began from the assertion, 'In the beginning was the Act', it soon appeared that the 'act' is theoretical, and its objective the achievement of a full self-consciousness.

The Critical philosophy, then, is an argument whose conclusion contradicts its major premiss. This premiss is the presupposition that reason is primarily theoretical. The conclusion is that reason is primarily practical. This is the general formal incoherence which comes to a head in the attempt to solve the antinomy of freedom. For it dictates the form in which the question is put; How can we determine, theoretically, a world in which we can act freely? The answer is, we have seen, that such a world cannot be determined by thought. Nevertheless, the real world is conceived *in terms of* the world which we *can* determine; but negatively, as a world which does not possess the particular determinateness which makes the world we know determinable; as a world which could be determined by a being not limited, as we are, by the need for a sensuous presentation, but capable of intellectual intuition. Thus the form in which Kant seeks to resolve the antinomy depends upon assuming the primacy of the theoretical standpoint. It is this which makes it necessary to conceive the problem as a relation between two possible objects of knowledge—two worlds—one of which *is* and the other *is not* determinable through our modes of cognition. It is not surprising, therefore—it is indeed inevitable—that the attempt should bring to light the underlying inconsistency and produce a palpable incoherence.

In this general inconsistency, this failure to decide between the primacy of the theoretical and the practical the Critical Philosophy points beyond itself. There is much to be said for the view that Kant's thinking, or at least his method of exposition, is dialectical: and this would be in full accordance with his acceptance of the romantic doctrine that thinking, *in concreto*, is a process of imaginative synthesis. Thinking is not limited to the production of knowledge. A system of transcendant metaphysics is a product of thinking; it is illusory only because, though not purely formal, it does not admit of verification by reference to experience. It is a familair point to students of the first *Critique*, that the doctrine of time expounded in the Aesthetic does not tally with the treatment of time in the Analytic; and that the most obvious reason for this lies in the method of exposition. For in the aesthetic we abstract completely from all conceptual elements; and in the analytic we discover that without concepts no experience whatever is possible. It follows that by excluding conceptual elements from consideration in the Aesthetic we make a complete account of time impossible, and what account is given at this stage must be amplified and qualified later on. But Kant does not rewrite the aesthetic in the light of the analytic, nor the analytic in the light of the dialectic. He proceeds from stage to stage by including elements of experience which have so far been left out of consideration; and consequently at each stage a more comprehensive synthesis is made possible, in which the contents of the earlier stages appear as elements. Yet the modification which they must undergo when so qualified by new considerations is left to the reader.

If we take this view of Kant's method of construction in the Critical Philosophy as a whole, we may resolve the formal contradiction between premiss and conclusion. Through every stage of the progressing argument Kant proceeds as if reason were primarily theoretical; as if the 'Cogito' and the standpoint it establishes were adequate. The conclusion, that reason is primarily practical, takes us beyond this premiss, and involves its qualification from a more comprehensive standpoint. But there is this difference from all earlier stages, that the discovery of the primacy of practical reason is a final conclusion, and not the starting-point of a new stage. Kant goes no further. Instead he erects a barrier against every attempt to go further. Our acceptance of practical reason and its categorical imperative remains a matter of faith. Our belief in freedom is a necessary but incomprehensible belief, and we can comprehend its incomprehensibility. We can indeed use its necessity as a basis for a reasonable hope that there is another life to bridge the gulf between duty and happiness, and a supreme being whose business it is to see that the gulf is bridged. Nevertheless, the Critical Philosophy points the way, even if it forbids the attempt, to a formal reconstruction which would start from the primacy of the practical, and take up into itself the theoretical as an element within the practical.

Before we carry this further we must consider the second

major criticism of the Critical philosophy, which is in respect of its adequacy. I have said that it is the most adequate of modern philosophies; but it is not *fully* adequate. It fails to do justice to that aspect of human experience of which religion is the reflective expression. It is true that in 1793 there appeared a treatise written by Kant under the title *Religion within the Bounds of Mere Reason*. But this work, for all its great merits, cannot be considered an integral part of the Critical philosophy. It is rather in the nature of an addendum to the *Critique of Practical Reason*. For it treats religion not as a distinct field of experience, grounded in a form of judgement which claims to be valid in its own right, but simply as a set of beliefs which are justifiable pragmatically in so far as they tend to support the rational will in its struggle against the incitements of inclination. There is indeed no room in the compact structure of the Kantian systematic, for a separate critique of religion. In the first *Critique* the proofs of the existence of God have been shown to be illusory, and in the religious field there can be no knowledge, and not even, in the logical sense, a *necessary* belief. The most that we can have is a reasonable hope, on the condition that we do our duty without regard to happiness in this world. Religion appears as a kind of justifiable mythology, concerned wholly with another life and another world; as a sop to the weakness of human nature or a crutch to aid the feebleness of our all too human wills. Above all Kant insists that religion must never be considered as the ground of morality. It is moral experience which provides the ground of religious belief.

Now whatever view we may hold about religion, this treatment of the subject cannot be regarded as a critical examination of the claims of religious experience. No great religious teacher could recognize in Kant's account anything that is of central significance to himself. St. Paul, in the Epistle to the Romans, comes in some ways close to Kant in his discussion of the moral law. 'I find then a law,' he writes, 'that when I would do good, evil is present with me. For I delight in the law of God after the inward man; but I see another law in my members, warring against the law of my mind, and bringing me into captivity to the law of sin which is in my members.'[1] But Paul's conclusion is very different. He answers Kant's question, 'If I do my duty, what may I hope?' by pointing to the impossibility of keeping the law. 'There is no difference. All have sinned and come short of the glory of God.'[2] The law can only judge and condemn us. St. Paul finds the significance of religion in being set free from the law of sin and death, as a matter of grace and not of desert. But we need not labour what is very obvious. How little evidence there is that Kant's discussion of religion has contributed anything to the purification of religious belief! How much reason there is for considering it one of the factors which have contributed to the idea that religion is unnecessary!

What concerns us, however, is not so much the inadequacy of Kant's treatment of religion, but the reason for it. It would not be enough, even if it were true, to suggest that Kant himself was not a deeply religious man. For an adequate intellectual critique of religious experience that would not be necessary. His treatment of aesthetic judgement is very adequate, yet there is no evidence that Kant was unusually sensitive to art. The adequacy in question is an intellectual adequacy, and the reason for it must be a formal one. The reason is that the adoption of the 'I think' as the centre of reference and starting-point of his philosophy makes it formally impossible to do justice to religious experience. For thought is inherently private; and any philosophy which takes its stand on the primacy of thought, which defines the Self as the Thinker, is committed formally to an extreme logical individualism. It is necessarily egocentric. Whether it is logically committed to solipsism we need not inquire. It may be so. But the point here is a purely formal one. It is simply that in recognizing the existence of a multiplicity of persons, it must treat them all as identical instances of the 'I think', whose differentiation is, for theoretical purposes, accidental. They must be represented as a multiplicity of 'I's. But it is a primary fact of experience that for each individual

[1] Romans vii, 21–3.   [2] Romans iii, 23.

person there is only one 'I'—himself. He cannot address another person as 'I' but only by means of the second personal pronoun 'You'. We may restate our criticism by saying, therefore, that any philosophy which takes the 'I think' as its first principle, must remain formally a philosophy without a second person; a philosophy which is debarred from thinking the 'You and I'.

Now the form of religious experience involves the distinction between the first and second persons. The idea of 'God' is the idea of a universal 'Thou' to which all particular persons stand in personal relation. The question of the validity of religious belief is a question of the validity of this form. Consequently, a philosophy which does not formally recognize the distinction between 'I' and 'You' cannot even formulate the religious problem; and a Critique of religion is thus rendered impossible. It must substitute for the second person an object which is thought to possess the characters by which we discriminate persons from things. God is then conceived as the supreme object of thought, and the knowledge of God must signify the determination of this object by means of the categories of the understanding. The necessary failure of this effort to categorize an infinite person is demonstrated by Kant in the Dialectic of the *Critique of Pure Reason*. But it was already a commonplace of theology; and it misses the point of religious experience totally, since the conception of God as the supreme object of the understanding is not a religious, but a pseudo-scientific conception.

But even if the universalization of the second person as an infinite Thou is invalid, this would not dispose of the problem. We should still have to inquire how the idea, valid or not, actually arises. For the formal distinction between 'I' and 'you' is not disposed of by the rejection of religion. What is generalized, legitimately or not, in the religious use of the term God, is a matter of empirical experience. It is our experience of personal relationship with one another. If we confine ourselves to the theoretical aspect of this—its aspect as knowledge, the form of the question is 'How do I know you?' It is not, 'How do I know that other "I"s exist?' The problem, therefore, which underlies any critique of religion is a problem of interpersonal knowledge. We may then reformulate our criticism of the adequacy of the Critical philosophy by saying that it fails to do justice to, and even to allow for the possibility of our knowledge of one another; and this failure arises because its formal conception of knowledge excludes this possibility by postulating the 'I think' as the primary presupposition of all experience.

These two criticisms of Kant's philosophy—of its formal coherence and its formal adequacy—have a common root. It is that any philosophy which takes the 'Cogito' as its starting point and centre of reference institutes a formal dualism of theory and practice; and that this dualism makes it formally impossible to give any account, and indeed to conceive the possibility of persons in relation, whether the relation be theoretical—as knowledge, or practical—as co-operation. For thought is essentially private. Formally, it is the contrary of action; excluding any causal operation upon the object which is known through its activity, that is to say, upon the Real. If we make the 'I think' the primary postulate of philosophy, then not merely do we institute a dualism between theoretical and practical experience, but we make action logically inconceivable—a mystery, as Kant so rightly concludes, in which we necessarily believe, but which we can never comprehend. However far we carry the process of thought it can never *become* an action or spontaneously *generate* an action. We may formulate the dualism in different ways, as a dualism of mind and body, of mind and matter, of theory and practice, of appearance and reality, of subjective and objective, of phenomenal and noumenal worlds, but we can never abolish it. Consequently I can never know another person, since thinking about another person can never amount to personal knowledge of him, nor even to personal acquaintance.

This may be clarified if I give here my reason for thinking that contemporary logical empiricism escapes from the range of the Critical philosophy, and belongs to a new emergent phase. My reason is that it shifts the locus of logical analysis from thought to language, and in doing so implicitly rejects the formal dualism which characterizes the two earlier periods of modern philosophy alike. For it substitutes for the 'I think' the 'I say', and thought becomes that aspect of speech which makes it intelligible—its logical structure. Speech is public. It is at once thought and action, or rather a unity of which 'mental' and 'physical' activity are distinguishable but inseparable aspects; and as a result it establishes communication, and introduces the 'you' as the correlative of the 'I'. For if the 'I think' logically excludes the second person, the 'I say' makes the second person a logical necessity. The 'I say' is logically incomplete. To complete it we must formulate it as follows: 'I say to you; and I await your response'. Thus the problem of the form of the personal emerges as the problem of the form of communication. Contemporary existentialism, which concerns itself with the matter of personal experience in its personal character, equally, and perhaps more consciously exhibits the emergence of the new problem. But here the problem shows a religious face. In the tension between its theistic and its atheist exponents it revolves around a religious axis, and formulates the problem of the personal in the antithesis, 'God—or Nothing'.

The final question, then, which the Critical philosophy leaves on our hands is this, 'Is it possible to take its conclusion —that reason is primarily practical—as the starting-point and centre of reference for a new effort of philosophical construction?' Can we substitute for the 'I think' the 'I do'? Kant insisted that we cannot. Is he justified in this? In the end the only answer must be to attempt it; the only refutation of Kant's negative must be to *do* it. For since the reason for Kant's denial lies in the acceptance of the 'Cogito' as his own centre of reference, it cannot be conclusive, and it may help us towards the effort we must make if we consider the 'Cogito' as it was originally formulated by Descartes, who established it as the starting-point of modern philosophy.

There is no need to consider any of the traditional criticisms of the Cartesian formula '*Cogito ergo sum*'. For the original assertion was intended to make a radical break with philosophical tradition and to establish a new starting-point. By its success it initiated a new philosophical tradition, and consequently all criticisms of it within the tradition which it established, are internal criticisms which depend upon its acceptance. They can only be criticisms of the manner of its formulation, not of what is formulated. The 'Cogito' establishes a new starting-point and centre of reference for philosophical reflection; it can only be challenged from outside the tradition it establishes, by establishing a different starting-point, with which it can be shown to be incompatible.

Historically, the 'Cogito' represents a challenge to authority and a declaration of independence; and so well did its author know this that he went in fear of the penalties that his boldness might incur. For Descartes it was equivalent to the assertion 'I am a substance whose essence is thinking'. If we eliminate the terms 'substance' and 'essence', which would limit its application to the first period of modern philosophy—(the second period substitutes the assertion 'I am a thinking organism')—we may paraphrase its significance for its time in the following way. 'I am a thinking being: to think is my essential nature. I have therefore both the right and the duty to think for myself, and to refuse to accept any authority other than my own reason as a guarantor of truth.' In this way the 'Cogito' constitutes an appeal from authority to reason.

In Descartes' own thinking the 'Cogito' appears as the conclusion of a systematic process of doubt. Unless interpreted in the light of this preliminary process, it loses a good deal of its significance. The method of doubt is the rejection of authority in operation. Within the body of tradition doubts of its authority had been growing for some centuries. Their social expression is the formation and spread of heretical sects which challenge the authority of the Church in matters of belief. This had been regarded as an evil, a disruption of social unity and a challenge to divinely established authority. The Church considered herself justified in taking the extremest measures for the suppression of heresy. Descartes, however, has systematized this doubt, and set it up as a canon for the proper employment of the intellect in the search for truth. This too has been accepted by modern thought, and it is now so familiar to us that we fail to recognize how paradoxical it is. Is it not *prima facie* unlikely that the effort to extend doubt systematically to the limits of possibility should issue in an extension of certainty? Is it not more likely that our capacity for scepticism is as unlimited as our credulity, and increases, like all our powers, with exercise. If, as a first result, we find something that we are unable to doubt, may this not signify merely that we have not doubted hard enough or systematically enough?

The method of doubt rests upon an assumption, which should be made explicit, that a reason is required for believing but none for doubting. The negative, however, must always be grounded in the positive; doubt is only possible through belief. If I find myself possessed of a certain belief, and know no reason for questioning it, I *cannot* doubt it; and if I could my doubt would be irrational. Moreover, if I do doubt one of my beliefs, then it is no longer a belief of mine, but only something that I used to believe.

It may be objected that this is to make an elementary mistake by confusing practical with theoretical doubt, and so failing to distinguish between logical certainty and psychological certitude. This is an internal objection, for the distinction itself derives from the method of doubt. In making the criticism we are indeed revealing the origin of the distinction between certainty and certitude, which is one aspect of the dualism of theoretical and practical which follows from the 'Cogito'. Since we are doubting—for good reasons—the adequacy of this standpoint, its implications have become problematical for us, and arguments which presuppose it are invalid. Belief and doubt are primarily practical; and from the standpoint of practical experience the distinction shows a different face. If in practice I believe, for instance, that I am surrounded by objects which have an independent material existence of their own, I can *pretend* to doubt this, without really doing so. If we call this a 'theoretical' doubt, we must beware lest the phrase misleads us into thinking that there are two species of doubt. A 'theoretical' doubt, in this usage, is an imaginary or non-existent doubt. When we talk about the lion and the unicorn we are not distinguishing two species of vertebrate animals. There are lions; there are no unicorns. We might agree to express the difference by calling unicorns 'theoretical' animals. But it would be foolish to conclude that there ought to be a science of 'theoretical' biology, and set out to explore systematically the rational structure of the world of theoretical organisms.

It cannot be true that I ought to doubt what in fact I believe, by a deliberate act of will. For this is an impossibility, and 'ought' implies 'can'. If then I am asked to adopt the method of systematic doubt, I am invited, as a matter of principle, to pretend to doubt what in fact I believe. What shall I gain by engaging in this game of make-believe? We are told that it is the proper way to start a systematic quest for the truth. In the end, it is hoped, we shall exchange our practical belief for a theoretical certainty. But what probability—I shall not ask what *certainty*—is there that this will be the result? Is it likely that a sustained effort of pretence will lead to knowledge? And if, by some happy chance, this theoretical certainty does emerge, what guarantee have I that it is not an imaginary certainty; and the knowledge which it certifies, a mere pretence of knowledge?

The method of doubt would have us abstract from the fact of belief or disbelief, separate what is believed from the believing of it and entertain it simply as a 'proposition' whose truth or falsity is undetermined. It is hoped that this will provide us with a neutral starting-point for an activity of thinking which aims to determine, purely theoretically, whether it is to be accepted as true or rejected as false. Only when it has been so certified by reason can it properly be said to be *known*. This, it may be said, is the point of view of philosophy—that nothing is known until it has been transformed, by rational criticism, from a mere belief into a logical certainty. Knowledge, in this strict sense of the term, is the product of thought and lies at the end of a process which begins in doubt.

We must reject this, both as standpoint and as method. If this be philosophy, then philosophy is a bubble floating in an atmosphere of unreality. Belief—not theoretical assent—is a necessary element in knowledge. A logical system of true propositions does not of itself constitute a body of knowledge. To constitute knowledge it must also be believed by someone. For knowledge cannot exist in the void; it must be *somebody's* knowledge. A proposition may be true even though no one believes it; but it cannot, until it is believed, be an element in *knowledge*. Suppose that I am presented with a triumphant logical demonstration. I accept its premisses; I can find no flaw in the argument. The conclusion follows with logical necessity and is therefore logically certain. But at the same time I find the conclusion impossible to believe. What then? I can only reject it *in toto*, even if I can find no theoretical grounds for doing so. This indeed was Hume's position in respect of Berkeley's philosophy. It admitted of no refutation, he said, yet it carried no conviction. And this proved, for Hume, that it was '*merely sceptical*'. If we take the method of doubt with complete seriousness, and the 'Cogito' which is already implicit in it, we must conclude, with some of our contemporaries, that all philosophy which is more than a logical analytic of language is 'nonsense'. We must leave all positive knowledge to the empirical sciences.

The particular unreality which concerns us is the disruption of the integrity of the Self through a dualism of practical and theoretical activity. We are asked to embark upon a purely theoretical activity which isolates itself from the influence of all 'practical' elements—since these must introduce bias and prejudice—in the hope of attaining a knowledge which will take precedence over the beliefs by which, in practice, we live. This, I say, is impossible in practice, and in conception self-contradictory. If we could so isolate our theoretical activities from practical influences—from the emotional motives, for example, and the intentional valuations which determine our behaviour, we should have destroyed our own integrity. We should need to become two selves, neither of which would be a complete self. There would be a 'practical' or 'bodily' self which acts without thinking, and a 'theoretical', 'spiritual' or 'mental' self, which thinks without acting. This is the genesis of the 'mind-body' problem, which is in fact no problem but a patent absurdity. How could we determine the relation between two entities which are themselves constituted by a postulate of unrelatedness? This disrupted self, consisting of a body and a mind incomprehensibly—that is, magically—united is happily described by Professor Ryle as 'the ghost in the machine'. We might comment, with advantage, that the machine is, of course, as imaginary as the ghost.

We can now understand why, in Descartes, the assertion of the 'Cogito' implies immediately both the definition of the Self as a thinking being, and the dualism of mind and matter. '*Cogito ergo sum*' in spite of its form, does not *infer* existence from thought. It identifies the two. Thought is the essence of my being. The dualism of mind and matter, again, is formally invalid, because it objectifies the distinction between subject and object, and so represents it as a distinction between two incompatible *objects* of thought. It is, in fact, the theoretical representation of the dichotomy between 'thinking' and 'acting', and in Kant's profounder analysis it appears in its proper form as a dualism of the theoretical and the practical. The point, however, which should be stressed is that the dualism arises, in whatever form, in the interest of the primacy of the theoretical. It follows from the definition of the Self as the Thinker. Consequently all philosophies which share the 'Cogito' as their starting-point, however they differ, have this in common, that they presuppose the primacy of the theoretical. They conceive reason at once as the differentia of the personal, as that which constitutes the human organism a 'self', and at the same time as the capacity for logical thought. Any philosophy which does this must find itself faced with the Kantian dilemma, 'How can pure reason become practical?' It was the impossibility of any answer that led Kant to conclude that reason is primarily practical; not primarily, that is to say, the capacity to think in terms of a distinction between 'true' and 'false' but to act in terms of a distinction between 'right' and 'wrong'.

We are now able to interpret the 'Cogito' in its essential significance, and in doing so to refute it. If thinking is my essence, then I am an active being—as Descartes, indeed, insists. '*Cogito ergo sum*,' then means, 'I am an agent, and my act is thinking.' Any other activities which may be ascribed to me are accidents, which must be excluded from my definition. My activity of thinking is what constitutes my existence. Now this is a contradiction in terms. Action is practical, and thinking denotes an activity which is not practical but purely theoretical. To exist is to have a being which is independent of thought; and what depends on thought for its being is no *thing* but a mere *idea*, like the unicorn. To say that it has an ideal existence is simply a confusion of categories, which can only mislead us. Unicorns do *not* have an ideal existence. They do not exist. There are no such things. To put it otherwise, to exist is to be part of the world, in systematic causal relation with other parts of the world. Thinking, however, is non-causal; it 'moves nothing'as Aristotle said. If it is an activity, it is an activity which is without effect in the realm of existence. If, with Descartes, I say that I am a thinking substance, I must go on to say with him that I am a totally insubstantial substance. In a word, in distinguishing between action and thought I distinguish between existence and non-existence. As an activity of thinking the Self appears as an activity which is no activity; as mind it appears as a substance which is no substance. Its existence, in a word, is a non-existence. In Kantian language we must recognize the 'Cogito' not as an element in existence, but as a transcendental unity of apperception, a formal, logical centre of reference; the primary postulate of the possibility of experience. But there is an advantage in keeping to the common-sense language of Descartes. If, in any sense, the fact that I am thinking proves—or should we say, presupposes—my existence, then it certifies my existence not as a mind, but as a body. If the actuality of my thinking reveals that I am an agent, my act cannot be an act of thought; for thinking can only be defined negatively in relation to a positive activity which is material, causal and effective in the modification of the not-self. It is an activity which is immaterial, and non-causal, having no effect in the existential determination of its object. If then I distinguish between action and thought, between the practical and the theoretical—as in some sense I must; and if I wish to use an existential language to mark the distinction, I must identify my existence with action; and my thinking with non-existence. I must say not '*Cogito ergo sum*', but '*Cogito ergo non-sum*'. What is to be made of this paradox we shall have to inquire later. It is easy to hide it by dressing it up in suitable words. One might say that thought transcends existence. We might speak of an existence beyond space and time, in an eternal present; or we might say, more simply that in thinking the self stands 'over against' the world which it knows. It is wiser not to use such devices for concealing our ignorance. The paradox is only the antinomy of freedom in another form. However we seek to resolve it, we may at least say this, that we can exhibit the '*Cogito ergo sum*' as self-contradictory because it asserts the primacy of the theoretical; while in truth, as Kant rightly concluded, it is the practical that is primary. The theoretical is secondary and derivative.

We may conclude these introductory chapters with a final comment on the Critical philosophy. The emergent problem, in the time of Kant, was the form of the organic. For constructive philosophy the task was to determine a logical schema of organic unity through which all experience might be coherently thought; or—to express it otherwise—to reject the Cartesian view that the Self is a substance and substitute for it the doctrine that the Self is an organism. Kant, however, set himself a critical task and raised a prior question. 'Is the organic form,' he asked in effect, 'and its subjective correlative, the standpoint of aesthetic intuition, adequate for the purpose?' His answer was a negative one. He set limits to the use of the new form. Beyond its validity as an instrument of knowledge lies a range of personal experience which is not amenable to it; and the effort to push it beyond its proper boundaries can only result in drowning morality and religion on the one hand, and true science on the other, in a flood of illusion. Freedom will be lost. Prudence in the pursuit of an all too human happiness will become the only standard of action. Knowledge, seeking to transcend its necessary limits, will be transformed into an illusory ideal. We must humbly recognize that the narrow circle of all possible human understanding is surrounded by unfathomable mystery. We must rest content in the conviction that what is real is forever beyond our ken.

We need not accept this scepticism as final. Philosophical scepticism is always formal; that is to say, it is relative to a particular form of thought. It arises from the discovery, through philosophical analysis, that the most adequate instrument of systematic thought which we possess is unable to represent our experience as a unity: and since the unity of experience is the correlate of the unity of the Self, this means that the form of our thought is inadequate for the comprehension of selfhood. Thus Hume's scepticism is a scepticism of the adequacy of the concept of substance, and so of the form of the material. The Self can not be conceived on the analogy of a material object. The scepticism of Kierkegaard—the most devastating of all modern scepticisms—is a criticism of the form of the organic in its fully developed Hegelian form. It means that the true Self cannot be conceived through the organic analogy. It is not an organic unity. Such scepticism is valid under a condition. It is valid only if the form in question is not merely the most inclusive form of understanding we yet possess, but the most inclusive form we can ever construct. This, however, can never be demonstrated. The answer to Hume's scepticism of the form of the material was the construction of the form of the organic. To the contemporary scepticism of the organic, the answer will be, if we can achieve it, the construction of the form of the personal. Such an instrument of thought would have a finality denied to the other two, for we should no longer be attempting to understand our human experience on the analogy of our knowledge of organisms or of physical substances, but directly, in terms of the personal character which is its own unique distinction.

Kant's scepticism, however, has a character of its own. It is a limited scepticism. As an outlook on life it is the formal definition of a sane, balanced and critical liberalism. Seen in retrospect it is a prophetic warning of the peril to freedom which lurks in the romantic outlook, the danger that the form of the organic will be used to plan and construct the good society on earth. For Kant himself his philosophy is a critical acceptance of Rousseau and the French Revolution. For us it is the prophetic analysis and condemnation of totalitarianism. We are aware today of the totalitarian implications of Rousseau's social theory, particularly in its mature development in Hegel. Totalitarianism is the result of determining the good as an object in the spatio-temporal world, and planning its achievement by the use of scientific techniques within a heuristic framework of organic concepts. Kant's condemnation of the attempt is this, that though it intends a free and self-determining society, it must necessarily result in destroying freedom, and with freedom morality and religion, so bringing human personality under the bondage of a total determination.

Kant could be content to limit knowledge and leave the beyond to faith and hope. For his time a dualism of theory and practice was possible, and indeed was the path of wisdom. For us it is impossible. We are committed to planning, whether we will or not, and planning is the unity of theory and practice under the primacy of the practical. So long as our most adequate concept is the organic concept, our social planning can only issue in a totalitarian society. This is the reason why the emergent problem of contemporary philosophy is the form of the personal. This is why we must disregard Kant's limitation, take the primacy of practical reason as our starting-point and eliminate dualism.

CHAPTER FOUR

Agent and Subject

Our introductory study had a twofold purpose; to determine objectively the problem for contemporary philosophy, and to discover how we must set about the task of solving it. The conclusion we have reached is that our problem is the form of the personal, and that we may hope to resolve it only by starting from the primacy of the practical. For we have seen that it is the assumption of the primacy of the theoretical in our philosophical tradition which institutes a formal dualism which cannot be resolved; that the basic form of this dualism is the division of experience into theoretical and practical, and that this dualism makes it impossible to think the unity of the Self and so to determine the form of a personal experience. We have, therefore, to begin by rejecting dualism through asserting the primacy of the practical.

What is here proposed is that we should substitute the 'I do' for the 'I think' as our starting-point and centre of reference; and do our thinking from the standpoint of action. Clearly we must ask at once what this can mean, and what are its implications? It may assist us in our attempts to answer this question if we notice that we cannot ask in advance whether this is possible. That can only be discovered in the attempt. For any reasoned objection to its possibility would presuppose the primacy of the theoretical, and would therefore be invalid. I emphasize this at the beginning because it provides the form of the answer to innumerable objections which must arise in our minds as we proceed. We must not underestimate the difficulty of the enterprise to which we are committed. We have to shift the centre of gravity in our philosophical tradition, and to alter our established mode of thinking. To propose this is easy; to accomplish it is so difficult that complete success at the first attempt is inconceivable. We are largely creatures of habit; not least in our reflective activities. To change our standpoint is to transform our habits of thought. It is not to exchange one theory for another, but to change the basis of all theory. To achieve this must, it seems to me, be a long, co-operative process; a stumbling advance in country where there are no beaten paths to follow, and where every step may lead us astray. No man, however great his intellectual powers might be, could trace all the ramifications of the process of readjustment, or avoid the tendency to relapse unconsciously into the familiar standpoint which he is seeking to overcome. I certainly have no confidence in my own ability to succeed; and I should relinquish the attempt unless I were convinced that we have no option but to try; and to hope that our failures will prove stepping-stones to final success.

The proposal to start from the primacy of the practical does not mean that we should aim at a practical rather than a theoretical philosophy. It may indeed have the effect of concentrating our attention upon action, as the primacy of the theoretical tends to concentrate attention upon the problems of knowledge. What it does mean is that we should think *from the standpoint of action*. Philosophy is necessarily theoretical, and must aim at a theoretical strictness. It does not follow that we must theorize from the standpoint of theory. Kant, one may recall, compared his change of standpoint to the Copernican revolution in astronomy. The present proposal might use the same analogy. Copernicus proposed to conceive the planetary system from the standpoint of an observer on the sun. This might seem at first sight, impossible, since the astronomer is necessarily upon the earth. Yet the objection is unfounded. Are we, as philosophers, in any worse case? We are indeed tied to an activity of reflection; but why should we be unable to reflect from the standpoint of action? Granted that in reflective activity the Self is subject, we need not conclude that we are debarred from thinking as though we were in action, and so from the standpoint of the Self as agent. This would indeed be impossible if there were an unbridgeable dualism between theory and practice; and from the standpoint of the 'Cogito' there is. Since this is our habitual standpoint in philosophical reflection, we are apt to think that the practical standpoint excludes the theoretical as the theoretical excludes the practical; or more naturally that we have a choice between a 'mentalist' and a 'materialist' systematic in theory; that we must either be 'realists' or 'idealists', and that which of the two we choose need make no difference *in practice*. But this reveals that we are still thinking from the theoretical standpoint. If we substitute for this the practical standpoint, the dualism between theory and practice disappears. Why this should be so is the first issue that requires clarification.

The Self that reflects and the Self that acts is the same Self; action and thought are contrasted modes of its activity. But it does not follow that they have an equal status in the being of the Self. In thinking the mind alone is active. In acting the body indeed is active, but also the mind. Action is not blind. When we turn from reflection to action we do not turn from consciousness to unconsciousness. When we act, sense, perception and judgement are in continuous activity, along with physical movement. When we think, we exclude overt bodily movement at least; what more we exclude depends upon the denotation we choose to give to the term 'thought', which in its usage is highly ambiguous. But perhaps we may say that the 'purer' our thought becomes, the more it excludes not merely perception, but all sensuous elements, and moves in a shadowy world of abstract and general ideas. Action, then, is a full concrete activity of the self in which all our capacities are employed; while thought is constituted by the exclusion of some of our powers and a withdrawal into an activity which is less concrete and less complete. Indeed, when we consider the contrast in this fashion, it tends to present itself as an abstract duality; in which action and thought are the positive and negative poles of a personal experience, which moves, in its actuality, between them. In a somewhat analogous fashion black and white present themselves as absolute contraries, though in reality they are the ideal limits of a series of grey tones. In the case of visual experience, too, one of the limits is positive and the other negative. Both are ideal limits; but while pure white is the complete fulness of light, black is its complete exclusion, so that the darker the tone the nearer we are to an exclusion of light, and so to the exclusion of the possibility of vision. A man born blind does not see only black. He does not see at all. It may indeed be said that this does not make white any more positive than black, since pure white means the total exclusion of darkness. This is true *in the abstract*. Yet, in fact, the exclusion of darkness is merely a double negative. It means the exclusion of the exclusion of light.

'Acting' and 'thinking' then, are, in abstract conception, exclusive contraries. In actuality they are ideal limits of personal experience; and 'acting' is the positive, while 'thinking' is the negative limit. This is what is expressed by the assertion of the primacy of the practical, or as Kant expressed it, the primacy of practical reason. The inclusion of the term 'reason' adds nothing essential. For what we are considering is personal experience, or the activity of the Self; and reason is the *differentia* of the personal. The concept of 'action' is *inclusive*. As an ideal limit of personal being, it is the concept of an unlimited rational being, in which all the capacities of the Self are in full and unrestricted employment. As limited and finite persons, such a fulness of positive being lies beyond our range. This does not affect the concept, but only its application to the particular case. The limitation marks the fact that we are never fully active, without restriction or qualification, in our experience as agents. The important issue, which is not an empirical one, is that 'action' without thought is a self-contradictory conception. We do indeed talk of 'acting without thinking'; but this again refers to empirical instances. It means that we acted without considering the relevant issues in a particular situation, that we acted without taking *proper* thought. It cannot mean that we acted with no thought at all; still less that we acted without ever having thought about anything. For only a thinking being could act without thinking. 'Thought', on the other hand, is an *exclusive* concept, and therefore negative. As an ideal limit—as 'pure' thought—it denotes an activity of the Self which is purely formal and completely without content. Now the purely formal is equivalent to nothing; for there cannot be a form which is not the form of something, and a purely formal activity is therefore an activity which is no activity. This, no doubt, is why we tend to say that when we are thinking we are doing nothing. 'Pure thought' is not merely impossible *for us*, it is impossible in the nature of things. It is not therefore, *as a concept*, self-contradictory, but merely secondary, derivative and negative; a concept formed by exclusion, and therefore relative to what is excluded. It is a necessary concept, since negation is necessary to thought. So, in pure mathematics, zero is a number, though it represents nothing. But the analogy of vision may help us better. We can report our experience of a pitch-black night either by saying that we see an unlimited darkness, or that we see nothing, or that we cannot see; and these three forms of statement are equivalent. But the first two are relative to our capacity to see and to our experience of seeing. If we had been born blind, only the third would be appropriate; but it would also be without meaning for us.

We should note here, if only to avoid possible misunderstanding as we proceed, that this implies a definition of 'action'. The term is loosely used, and can give rise to serious ambiguity. We talk of the actions of animals; we even refer to the action of an acid upon a metal. When we use the term in this way, we are employing an anthropomorphic metaphor. There is no objection to this, for such looseness is essential to the proper functioning of language. But we should be aware of what we are doing, especially when we are engaged upon an abstract inquiry. In the strict sense of the term only a person can 'act', or in the proper sense '*do*' anything. If this is not agreed, I shall not argue the point. It is sufficient for the present purpose to say that in this inquiry we shall use the term 'action', and the other terms which are its derivatives and synonyms, in this sense. We are concerned with personal activities, with the agency of the Self. In this context, action and thought both imply rationality. We may, however, use the term 'activity' without this implication, as a generic term with a wider significance, so that we can distinguish both thought and action as modes of rational activity. As a further aid to definition we may add that action is activity in terms of the distinction between 'right' and 'wrong', and that thought is activity in terms of the distinction between 'true' and 'false'.

With these points clear we can go a step farther. If the concept of 'pure thought' is derived from the concept of action by exclusion, then thought, so far as it is actual, falls within action, and depends upon action. Action is primary and concrete, thought is secondary, abstract and derivative. This must mean that the distinction between 'right' and 'wrong', which is constitutive for action, is the primary standard of validity; while the distinction between 'true' and 'false' is secondary. In some sense, though not necessarily directly, it must be possible to distinguish between 'right' and 'wrong' before distinguishing between 'true' and 'false', and so without reference to the truth or falsity of a judgement, and to derive the latter from the former. In other words, a theory of knowledge[1] presupposes and must be derived from, and included within a theory of action.

We may now formulate our starting-point more clearly. We have to substitute for the 'I think' as our centre of reference, the 'I do'. The 'I think' is not ultimate; it is the negative mode of the activity of the Self, and presupposes the 'I do'. For one possible answer to the question 'What are you doing?' is that I am thinking. We must, therefore, conclude that the 'I do' is

---

[1] I use the term 'theory of knowledge' in a very general sense; such that any attempt to determine the distinction between 'true' and 'false' implies a theory of knowledge.

the primary principle which is presupposed in all our experience; and that 'acting' and 'thinking' are opposite modes of 'doing', acting being the positive and thinking the negative mode. The Self, then, is not the thinker but the doer. In its positive doing it is agent; in its negative doing it is subject. We shall distinguish these two fundamental concepts by calling the one the concept of the Self-as-subject, and the other the concept of the Self-as-agent.

Our next step must be to determine more definitely the relation between the Self-as-agent and the Self-as-subject. The formal relation of a positive to the negative which is derived from it by exclusion is still too abstract. But this abstract distinction falls within the unity of the Self. It is the same Self that is both agent and subject. Now the logical correlate of the Self is the Other, and we shall have to use this distinction of Self and Other later on. But for the moment let us employ a more common term, and speak of the Other as the world. We may then say that, since the world is the correlate of the Self, the world in which the Self, as agent, acts, is the same world which as subject, it knows.[1]

It might appear, however, that this assertion of the primacy of the Self as agent, has been achieved through a mere verbal transposition. Must we not raise a prior question, 'How do we *know* that the self is agent?' Clearly if this question is logically prior, then the primacy of the practical cannot be maintained. But the question only seems to be a prior question from the standpoint of the Self as subject. The answer is simply that if, when acting, we did not know that we were acting we would *not* be acting. If any occurrence is to be an act of mine, I must know that I perform it. This, indeed, is the meaning of the statement that action, in distinction from thought, is an inclusive concept. To do, and to know that I do, are two aspects of one and the same experience. *This* knowledge is absolute and

[1] Even Kant, in spite of his distinction betsween a phenomenal and a noumenal world, could not take exception to this, since the phenomenal world is the noumenal world as it appears to the Subject.

necessary. It is not, however, knowledge of an object but what we may call 'knowledge in action'.

Consider now the Self in relation to the world. When I act I modify the world. Action is causally effective, even if it fails of the particular effect that is intended. This implies that the Self is part of the world in which it acts, and in dynamic relation with the rest of the world. On the other hand, as subject the Self stands 'over against' the world, which is its object. The Self as subject then is not part of the world it knows, but withdrawn from it, and so, in conception, outside it, or other than its object. But to be part of the world is to exist, while to be excluded from the world is to be non-existent. It follows that the Self *exists* as agent but not as subject.

We can now understand how the antithesis of matter and mind originates. Matter, like most of our fundamental concepts, is a practical conception. It signifies originally, like the corresponding terms in Greek and Latin, ὕλη and *materia*, the stuff of which something is made. The reference is to the technical activities of craftsmen. Clay is the matter or material from which the potter makes his pots. In general, therefore, matter is that which is acted upon, or that which has form imposed upon it by an agent. Formed matter we call 'body'. Now since nothing can be acted upon which offers no resistance, that is to say, which does not react upon the agent, the agent must himself be material. As agent, therefore, the Self is the body. Conversely the Self, as subject, is the mind. For as subject, the Self is non-agent, withdrawn from action, and, therefore, non-body. Since the Subject is the negative aspect of the Self, all characterizations of the Self as subject participate in its negativity and must be defined by reference to practical experience. This is the reason why the terms which we use to denote or describe 'mental' or 'subjective' processes and activities were originally and often still are used with reference to practical experience and its objects. It is often said that they are used metaphorically when applied to the theoretical world. But if so, they are not ordinary metaphors. They are practical expressions used, as it were, with a negative sign attached. The unicorn is a non-existent animal; and when we make a mental note of something, we make a note which is not, in fact, made. Thus as an agent I am a body, operative, material and existent; as a subject I am a mind, causally ineffective, immaterial and non-existent.

These verbal paradoxes, now that their significance has been explained, will, I hope, no longer sound foolish or shocking. They are formal and conceptual. They are rooted in the fact that to think is to discriminate, and the bare form of discrimination is the distinction between positive and negative. They do, however, set a logical problem which requires consideration. We must ask how the relation of the Self as agent to the Self as subject is to be logically construed. This is indeed the problem of the logical form of the personal. But before we can attempt an answer, we must consider shortly what is meant by a logical form.

Logic itself is a highly problematical discipline. That in some sense it is formal, no one doubts; but form is essentially relative, and any form must be the form of something. A pure form, in an absolute sense, is a pure nothing. But when we ask, 'What is it that "has" the form which the logician seeks to determine?' we face the problem of logic. For to this question different answers have been given; and in consequence different 'logics' have been constructed which are incompatible with one another. I have in mind, in particular, the difference between idealist or dialectical logic and realist or formal logic. The dialectical logic of the idealists—I should describe it myself as the logical form of the organic—is derived from Kant's transcendental logic, by suppressing, in the manner I have already described, part of Kant's own logical doctrine, which the developing organic concept considered to be the persistence of a pre-critical view which Kant had failed to overcome. For Kant maintained that the traditional formal logic was an *a priori* science, like pure mathematics, and considered therefore that his transcendental logic was quite compatible with it. The idealists considered them incompatible. May it not be that Kant was right in this instance as in others? If so, it must mean that idealist and formal logicians are studying the forms of different things.

Consider first, from the standpoint of the 'I do', the procedure of mathematics. If I have a practical problem which admits of an algebraic solution, I have a double task before me. I must first formulate the relevant aspects of the concrete situation in a set of algebraic equations. When I have done this, I must go on to solve the equations by a procedure which is dictated by rules for the manipulation of algebraic symbols. These two tasks, though interrelated, are distinct. The first demands a concrete grasp of an actual situation, and consists in constructing a symbolic representation of the situation, or of that part of it which is relevant to the problem. The second is a series of transformations of the symbolic representation in accordance with general rules, and requires no understanding of the situation which is formally represented. It can indeed be done for me by someone else, or by a machine constructed for the purpose.

Now any actual activity of thinking involves these two processes, or at least their analogues. It involves, firstly, a constructive process of symbolization, usually in words. This is much more than a mere description; for it involves relevant selection and combination. Secondly, it involves the drawing of inferences, for which the symbolic representation provides the premisses. Any actual process of inference presupposes a combination of premisses. Once the premisses have been combined in the requisite fashion, the conclusion follows of necessity, though it may not always be obvious what it is that is implied. This part of the thinking is a manipulation of symbols according to rules, and with a knowledge of the rules and a suitable symbolic system, it can be accomplished by a machine. But for the selection and combination of the premisses no rules can be given. The importance of this in the discovery of the unknown is apt to be overlooked if we limit our attention to the process of proof or demonstration. For when we prove or demonstrate a proposition the conclusion of the inference is already known, and this dictates the selection of premises from which it can be inferred. Proof is a secondary and derivative process. But a set of facts may be quite well known, and yet their implications remain undiscovered. Some of them may be known to one person, the others to another; or all may be known to the same individual. But nothing follows from them unless they are 'thought together' in the requisite form.

The logician can take either of these two formal aspects of thought as the central problem of his science. He may construct a logic which is concerned with the forms of inference, and so with the rules for the manipulation of a linguistic symbolism. The problem of the form of representation he may consider to lie outside his province; and the simplest way of doing this is to take language as a presupposition, and appeal to the common modes of speech to settle questions which concern the propriety of linguistic usage. On this side, the business of logic will arise from the deficiencies of ordinary language—its ambiguities and looseness of structure, and will consist in devising a symbolic system which will not be subject to such defects, and which will lend itself, like a mathematical symbolism, to exact manipulation in accordance with unambiguous rules.

Now this aspect of logical theory is not problematic. It does not give rise to fundamental controversy between different types of logic. But if the logician concentrates his attention upon the other aspect—upon the adequacy of the forms of representation which the process of formal inference must presuppose—the case is different. The logic of implication determines the form of the relation between a conclusion and its premises. It makes it possible to determine, by a formal analysis, whether a particular conclusion is or is not correctly inferred from the combination of certain premises. But it has nothing to say about the *truth* of the conclusion, unless the truth of the premises is presupposed. This is not solely a material question. It has its formal aspect. For the premises themselves are symbolic constructions. Propositions are not data; they are formulations of what is given in a concrete experience. This formulation involves the analysis of something that is given as a unity. The elements distinguished have to be represented by symbols, and their unity must be represented by a pattern of relations which binds the symbols together into a whole. Such a unity-pattern, as we may call it, is synthetic, theoretical and formal. It is therefore a logical form for the representation of the actual unity of the object to which our thought refers; that is to say, the unity which is apprehended in practical experience, which is not necessarily synthetic, and which is necessarily neither theoretical nor formal. It was with this form of representation that Kant was concerned in his transcendental logic, and since his day a unity-pattern of this kind has often been referred to as a system of categories.

Now a logic of the form of representation, unlike the logic of implication, is problematical. For it gives rise to the question whether there is only one unity-pattern—one system of categories—or more than one; and if so which of them is the most adequate for the representation of Reality: which means ultimately, as we have seen, for the representation of the unity of the Self. It is on this issue that the difference between the dialectical logic of modern idealists and the formal logic of the realists, properly rests, though this is apt to be obscured by the failure to distinguish clearly between the two aspects of logical form. Formal logic, at least in its developed modern form, assumes, even when it does not assert, the exclusive adequacy, for all knowledge, of the mathematical unity-pattern, which represents the unity of the object as a summation of identical elements. The dialectical logic, however, rests upon the doctrine that this pattern is inadequate to represent the unity of a directed process, such as is recognized in all living creatures. It offers instead an organic unity-pattern, in which the elements are qualitatively different, and functionally related by their complementary contributions to a unity of development.[1]

[1] The characterizations of the unity patterns are approximate only, but sufficient for the present purpose. A further treatment of the subject may be found in an earlier work of mine, *Interpreting the Universe* (Faber and Faber, 1933).

We may now return to the question which we formulated earlier. How is the relation of the Self as agent to the Self as subject to be construed logically? In other words, How can we represent formally the unity of the Self in its two modes of activity? The crux of this problem lies, as we have seen, in this, that formally the Self as subject is the negation of the Self as agent, and since it is by its own activity that the Self withdraws from action into reflection, its subjecthood is its self-negation. Thus the unity of the Self is a unity of self-affirmation and self-negation.

Such a unity can be represented neither in a mathematical nor in a dialectical form. For in the mathematical form positive and negative exclude one another. The rule of representation is that everything must be represented as always identical with itself. This is necessary because the pure form is a relation of identities, and therefore all differences in the real must be represented by differences in the relations between elements, while the elements themselves remain unaffected by any change in their relations to one another. Consequently, the unity of a positive and its negative is unthinkable. The sum of $+a$ and $-a$ is always zero. Positive and negative cancel one another out. If then we attempt to represent the Self through the mathematical unity-pattern, the result is necessarily a dualism of mind and body, that is to say, of the Agent-self and the Subject-self. The Self can be represented either as a physical system, or as a mental system, and these two systems exclude one another. Yet both are necessary. The unity of the two must be postulated, but cannot be represented. It must be postulated because without a relation between the 'mental' and the 'physical' systems neither knowledge nor action is possible.

The organic form might seem to be in a better position; and indeed it has the advantage that it can represent the spontaneity of the Self, and to this extent is more adequate. Moreover it can represent a unity of positive and negative elements, which stand in a necessary dialectical relation as thesis and antithesis in the unity of a process of development. If then we

conceive the Self not as substance but as organism, and represent it through the organic unity-pattern, it might appear that
its positive and negative modes, as agent and as subject, could
be represented as thesis and antithesis in a dialectical process of
self-development. But this is an illusion. For thesis and antithesis represent successive phases in the development of a unitary system. If we represent action and thought as thesis and
antithesis in a self-development, we must represent them as
successive phases in the development of the Self. But then it
must be impossible to represent the same Self as *at one and the
same time* both Agent and Subject. For when it is Agent it will
not be Subject; and if this were actually the case, then the Self
could never know that it was Agent, nor could it ever act with
knowledge. The positive and negative phases would still exclude
one another, and no synthesis would be possible. This, we may
recall, is precisely Kierkegaard's criticism of the Hegelian philosophy. The dialectic of the personal life, he maintains, is a
dialectic without a synthesis.

The result of this inadequacy of the organic unity-pattern is
that again it gives rise to a philosophical dualism. The Self may
be represented either as a developing organic system of thought,
or as a developing organic system of action. Either a dialectical
idealism or a dialectical materialism becomes possible, but no
unity of the two. When Karl Marx set out to make the Hegelian
social philosophy practical, declaring that philosophers hitherto
have only explained the world, while the task is to change it, he
could claim that he had merely inverted the dialectic. He found
it standing on its head, he asserted, and turned it right side up.
He did this by substituting the Self as 'worker' for the Self as
'thinker', without changing the organic unity-pattern. The
result is a dialectic of the practical in place of a dialectic of the
theoretical life.

Neither the form of the material, nor the form of the organic
is adequate to represent the unity of the Self. But by discovering
the ground of their inadequacy we make it possible to recognize
the structure which must be required in an adequate form of

representation. The unity of the Self is neither a material nor an organic, but a personal unity. The logical form of such a unity is one which represents a necessary unity of positive and negative modes. The Self is constituted by its capacity for self-negation. It must be represented as a positive which necessarily contains its own negative.

A formal conception of this sort is at once so abstract and so foreign to our traditional modes of thought that it will seem incomprehensible until it is referred to the types of experience which render it necessary. The necessary references will be given progressively in the sequel. But it is desirable to suggest at once some of the problems of personal experience which appear, *prima facie*, to possess such a form. The most familiar is no doubt the experience which we refer to as the moral struggle. From the time of Plato at least this has been both a commonplace of the moralists and a constant obstacle to the intellectual effort to represent the self as a unity. Constituent elements in our nature seem to be at war with one another. There is an active and dynamic contradiction between desire and reason, between flesh and spirit, between the 'law in my members', and 'the law of my mind'. Different elements within us seem to be in competition with one another for the control of behaviour. Attempts to describe the relation between these elements in the Self tend to deny the unity which they seek to analyse, by lending to the parts the characters which properly belong only to the whole. The one Self becomes two selves—a higher self and a lower self, a controlling self and a self that is to be controlled. We have to learn to control ourselves, yet the very conception of self-control is paradoxical, for, as Plato pointed out, the man who is master of himself is thereby also slave of himself. The fact of experience that is expressed in all this is that the unity of the Self contains, and indeed is constituted by a practical contradiction between its elements.

Another puzzling example is our capacity for self-deception. Again the fact is undeniable, yet the effort to think it seems to lead to absurdity. To deceive myself can only mean to persuade myself to believe what I know to be untrue. This seems a plain impossibility, yet we constantly find that we have accomplished it. We repress unacceptable desires, and censor our own thoughts, so that they are prevented from coming to consciousness. How is this possible unless we are conscious of them? To think this is to think a consciousness which contains the unconscious as a constituent element.

Consider finally a group of difficulties which more closely concern the business of philosophy. In the field of the personal the attempt at definition meets with peculiar difficulties. If, with Aristotle, we define Man as a rational organism, we have to reckon with the fact that very few men behave, or even think, with any high degree of rationality. We find one another, if not ourselves, rather unreasonable creatures. Yet this fact does not vitiate the definition, because only a rational being can behave irrationally. Philosophy is therefore driven to distinguish between the rational and the irrational elements in the Self, and both are then constituents of its unity. The irrational element is necessary to the constitution of the rational whole.

This difficulty of definition faces us whenever we try to give an account of any mode of personal activity. In the Theaetetus, for instance, Plato pointed out that the difficulty in giving an account of knowledge, is that it is a false account unless it allows for the possibility of error. How can we think falsely? For the capacity to think is the capacity to draw correct conclusions from given premises. In that case, if we draw incorrect conclusions we are not thinking. Yet a thinking that could not be incorrect could not be correct either; and thinking is an activity in terms of the distinction between true and false. To think is indeed to discriminate between what is incorrectly and what is correctly thought. If I could not think wrongly I could not think at all. Though I must *define* thinking as thinking truly, there can *be* no thinking which does not need its own negation to constitute it.

It is the same in ethics. Morality is doing the good. There is no problem here; the problem of morality is the problem of evil.

An account of morality, to be a true account, must show how evil is possible. To do this it must show that evil is both real and necessary. In fact most ethical theories represent evil either as necessary but unreal; or as real but unnecessary, and so they fail as theories. Morality is acting in terms of a distinction between good and evil. We can define it only in terms of doing good, or acting rightly. But in its reality as an experience it is otherwise. The problem that faces us when we seek to do what is right is the impossibility of doing it without an admixture of what is wrong. In actual practice, the good includes its negation in its own constitution. So Kant rightly pointed out that for a pure will duty could not exist.

These examples may perhaps suffice for the moment. We shall conclude our formal exposition by attempting to express the meaning of this logical form—of a positive which includes and is constituted by its own negative—in four propositions which though still formal, are not purely logical, but indicate the reference of the pure form to our actual experience. The first proposition is as follows:

1. *The Self is agent and exists only as agent.*

This proposition requires no further comment, since the first part of the chapter was concerned to expound it. It is the positive assertion which defines the existential character of the Self. We may pass therefore to the second proposition, which is concerned with the negative aspect which is excluded from the definition. It runs as follows:

2. *The Self is subject but cannot exist as subject. It can be subject only because it is agent.*

This proposition summarizes what we have already discussed in considering the relation between knowledge and action. There cannot be a pure subject, since this is the pure negation of agency, and a self which does not act cannot exist. The Self-as-subject is the Self conceived negatively, as the Self in its non-existence. An activity of pure thought is a non-existent activity; that is to say, it is a mere idea, though a necessary idea, and in no sense illusory. Illusion only enters if we posit it as an existent. When therefore we indicate the experience to which the idea refers, we have to point to the fact that the Subject can exist only as an aspect of the Self as agent. It is the negative aspect of the existence of the Agent. In other words, thought is at once the contrary of action and something that we do.

This brings us to the third proposition, which, with the fourth, concerns the functional, rather than the existential relation between the agency and the subjecthood of the Self. It is this:

3. *The Self is subject in and for the Self as agent.*

We have already indicated that the negative aspect of the personal is included in its existence, that is, in action. Now since action is deliberate activity which intends a change in the Other, its negative aspect is included in this intention; and consequently it is not merely *in* action but also *for* action. This signifies that knowledge, in its primary aspect at least, arises in action; that is to say, in an activity which does not *aim* at knowledge. If then we mean by 'thinking' an activity which aims at knowledge, it is not true that knowledge in general is the result of thinking. On the contrary, thinking presupposes knowledge. Our knowledge of the world is primarily an aspect of our action in the world. This indeed is reflected in the fact that our knowledge of the truth of a conclusion depends upon a prior knowledge of the truth of its premisses. We can only think about what we already know. This primary knowledge is the knowledge that arises in action, apart from any theoretical intention. It is this knowledge to which we sometimes refer when we use— somewhat ambiguously—the term 'experience'; as when we say that we know 'by experience' that Great Britain is an island. What we mean is that going to the continent from this country involves crossing the sea. It is worth noting that this piece of knowledge is *theoretically* an empirical generalization and therefore hypothetical. In reality it is absolutely certain.

The proposition means also that theoretical activities, in which the intention is knowledge, fall within action and have an essential reference to action. The reference may, of course, be indirect and in a sense must always be so. Sometimes this activity of reflection may be a subordinate activity falling within a practical intention, as when I have to stop and think before I can proceed with what I am doing. Sometimes, however, we reflect simply in order to know; and our third proposition does not deny this. What it asserts is that if the result of reflection is knowledge, if the theoretical conclusion can be significantly true or false, then it can function as a determinant in action, and modify the form of action, whether in a particular case it does so or not; and this is not accidental, but essential to the constitution of knowledge. In other words, the question which a theoretical activity seeks to answer can only arise in practical experience, directly or indirectly; and the answer can be true or false only through a reference to action. Thought cannot provide a criterion of truth, but at most a criterion of the correctness of the process of thinking.

The fourth proposition is in a sense the converse and complement of this. We may formulate it as follows:

4. *The Self can be agent only by being also subject.*

We may expand this by noticing first that the existence of the Self is its agency. The existence of the Self therefore, according to this fourth proposition, depends upon its capacity to be subject and as such, not agent. We have already expressed this by saying that the Self exists in virtue of its own self-negation. At the limit of abstraction there is an identity of action and reflection. To act and to know that I am acting are two aspects of one experience; since if I did not know that I was acting I should not be acting. And since to act is to do something, I must know to some extent what I am doing if I am doing it. There cannot be action without knowledge. Yet action is logically prior to knowledge, for there can be no knowledge without an actual activity which supports it; but there can be actual activity without knowledge. Such activity however is not action, but only movement; or at most reaction to stimulus; not a deliberate effort to modify the Other.

CHAPTER FIVE

The Perception of the Other

W e have now determined our standpoint. It is the standpoint of the Agent. We have also determined the logical form of the personal as one in which a positive contains and is constituted by its own negative. A self, we have said, is a being that exists through self-negation. Our task now is to give to this pure form a progressively more concrete content. For this purpose we ought first to consider the character of sense-perception from the standpoint of the Self as agent. For in some form sense-perception is fundamental to all our experience, and constitutes a 'given' both for thought and for action. From the standpoint of the 'Cogito', which establishes a dualism of mind and body, sense perception is a mystery, because as sense it is bodily while as perception it is mental. Descartes was clear about this, and saw that sense-perception must be excluded from the process of thought. If we presuppose the 'Cogito', then knowledge, if it is to be truly knowledge, must start from concepts and proceed through concepts. But since Locke, or at least since Kant, it has been recognized that this is impossible. Yet the problem remains, so long as the primacy of the theoretical is assumed. Attempts to make sense-perception the basis of knowledge, as in some sense it clearly is, must either assimilate the material to the mental, or absorb the mental in the material.

Theories of sense-perception have always tended to be primarily theories of vision. I am referring, of course, to philosophical theories. Scientific theories of sense-perception are out of court, since they must presuppose the issue that is at question. Indeed they are characteristically self-refuting; because as scientific they assume that in normal sense-perception we apprehend material objects in space, and as theories of sense-perception they conclude that we do not, but are aware only of the effects of these material objects upon our bodily organs. An inquiry which limits itself to tracing the transformations of energy through the nervous system from a receptor organ to a muscular contraction is debarred from including in the circuit any element of a 'mental' character. There is no place in the system for it. The philosophical problem of sense-perception is how we apprehend the existence of such energy transformations in the first place, and indeed what ground we have, other than an inexplicable natural belief, for thinking that they have an independent existence at all. Philosophical theories of perception, I have said, tend to be theories of visual perception. They assume the primacy of vision: that is to say, they take vision as the model of all sensory experience, and proceed as though it were certain that a true theory of visual perception will apply, *mutatis mutandis*, to all other modes of sense-perception.

Now this concentration of attention on vision has had very important effects upon philosophy in general. From the time of the Greeks, and especially through the influence of Plato, 'vision' has tended to be the model upon which all *knowledge* is construed. Thought is taken to be an inner vision. Reflection is 'contemplation'. The basis of science is 'observation', and the scientist himself is 'the observer'. When we talk of the world which we discover in sense-perception as the world which we come to understand by reflective thought, we usually mean the world that we see when we use our eyes. This tendency, of course, is not merely a philosophical convention. It has powerful roots in the *de facto* importance of vision in practical life. But if we are seeking an adequate theory of sense-perception it is dangerous to give way to such psychological tendencies, however natural. The most serious effect of doing so is that visual experience will tend to provide the model for the apperception

"The imperialism of the eye"

of the Self as subject. If we construe the Subject as the observer, then in knowledge the Self, as subject, 'stands over against' the object which it knows, and any activities involved in this knowing must be purely subjective, or mental; that is to say, they make no difference to, or have no causal effect upon, the object. The influence of the visual model is very clear in this. In visual perception we do stand over against the object we see; it is set before us, and our seeing it has no causal effect upon it. Seeing is *prima facie* a pure receptivity; to exercise it attentively, we withdraw from action altogether. We stop to look. In consequence, the visual model tends to instigate a strong contrast between knowing and acting, which in abstract theory passes easily into a conceptual dualism.

What concerns us now is not a theory of perception for its own sake, but an answer to the question, 'How is it that through sense-perception I am aware of the Other?' I say 'the Other' and not the Object; because the object is the correlative of the subject, and we must avoid this when we adopt the standpoint of action. The Self as agent is an existent, and its correlative therefore, is also in existence. It is this correlative of the Agent-self that I refer to as the Other. In a particular case the Other may be another thing or another organism or another person. In referring to the Other we abstract from these differentiations, and attend only to the general characteristic of being an existent other than the existing Self. Our question is therefore, 'How do we come by our awareness of existents other than ourselves?' From the standpoint of the 'Cogito' no answer is possible. The Object, as correlative of the Subject, carries no implication of existence, since the Subject is not itself, as subject, an existent. The Object is simply whatever I think about when I think. Nor is there any way from thought to existence. No judgement can discriminate between existence and non-existence in the object of thought; for as Kant showed, existence is not a predicate. It follows that the only viable type of philosophy, from the standpoint of the 'Cogito', is idealism; and I must agree with the realist criticism that all idealism is subjective idealism, which in turn must reduce to solipsism. But the realist assertion that what is perceived by the senses is not dependent on the mind seems also to be a sheer dogma. At most the realist can assert that what is apprehended in sense-perception is not *necessarily* dependent on the perceiving of it. The independent existence of the object remains problematical. It is a possibility for which no evidence can be offered.

But from the standpoint of the Agent the case is different. We are not here concerned with sense-perception as a lower limit of thought, but as an element in action. The form of action includes knowledge as its negative; for without perception action could not be. It is this that makes it necessary to consider sense-perception afresh, and in particular, to avoid the assumption that visual perception is primary. For such an assumption suggests that all forms of perception are, as vision *prima facie* seems to be, a pure receptivity to impressions.

That this is not so can best be seen by contrasting visual with tactual perception. The fundamental difference is that tactual perception involves physical contact between the organ of sense and the object perceived, while vision is incompatible with this. Sight operates only at a distance, touch only in contact. But this must be stated otherwise if its full significance is not to be missed. I can only become aware of anything tactually by doing something to it. Tactual perception is *necessarily* perception in action. To touch anything is to exert pressure upon it, however slight, and therefore, however slightly, to modify it. Visual perception, on the contrary, excludes any operation upon its object, and is a perception in passivity.

Now if we ask which of these modes of perception, the active or the passive, takes priority of the other as the basis of knowledge, the answer must be that touch is prior to vision. A man may be born blind and yet grow up to know the world he lives in and to direct his activities by this knowledge. His lack of vision is a great limitation and a serious handicap, but it does not take away his capacity for objective knowledge. But is it possible to conceive a human being who never possessed a tactual sense? It is of course possible to imagine this, in the sense that it is possible to imagine anything that is compatible with the conditions of intuition. It is possible to imagine a centaur, or even to paint a recognizable picture of a centaur; and even to believe in the creature's existence, so long as one does not ask questions about its physiology. Indeed when we imagine the existence of a pure subject we are precisely imagining a being possessed of a merely passive intuition, of the type of visual perception. But any question about how such a being, if he were born into the world without the capacity to feel any pressure upon him, could survive; or if he could survive, how he could ever know that he was surrounded by a world of things, reveals that the situation is unthinkable. The theoretical reason for this is that a purely visual experience would provide no ground for distinguishing in practice between imagining and perceiving. The result would be a practical solipsism.

The core of tactual perception is the experience of resistance. Now resistance is not a sense-datum, even if it may perhaps include as part of the experience what may be abstracted as such. It is essentially a practical experience. By this I mean that it presupposes that I am doing something, that I am in action, and that I am prevented from achieving my intention. If, *per impossibile*, I could be totally passive, and still conscious, I should be totally incapable of experiencing resistance. Resistance, therefore, is a frustration of the will. The experience occurs only when I am prevented from doing something that I am trying to do. If, for example, I set about walking straight forward in the dark, and collide with a wall, I become aware of the wall as an obstacle to my progress. The harder I press forward, the stronger the resistance. Yet if I had stopped walking before I reached the obstacle, I should never have known that it was there.

Now since my existence in general is my being an agent, because the 'I do' is the centre of origin of all my experience, it follows that my momentary existence is identified for me with what I am doing at the moment. The tactual experience of resistance is the experience of something, not myself, which prevents me from doing what I am doing. Tactual perception, as the experience of resistance, is the direct and immediate apprehension of the Other-than-myself. The Other is that which resists my will. Moreover, if we limit our experience to the mere experience of resistance alone, then we must say that it reveals to us that the Other exists, but not at all what it is. The Other appears simply as the negation of the Self, as that which limits its existence. It is that which moves against me, in the negative direction.

Since we are referring to personal experience, we shall expect to find that it includes and is constituted by its own negative. Notice first that I might, for instance, have chosen as example a man's effort to stand still and upright in the teeth of a gale. In that case the resistance would be his resistance to an active force compelling him to move against his will. He is then aware of himself as that which resists the Other. The fact that we can exemplify the experience of resistance either way shows us that in practical experience Self and Other are correlatives discriminated together by their opposition; and this opposition constitutes the unity of the experience. The Self does not first know itself and determine an objective; and then discover the other in carrying out its intention. The distinction of Self and Other is the awareness of both; and the *existence* of both is the fact that their opposition is a practical, and not a theoretical opposition. For if we posit the primacy of the theoretical, the distinction would fall within the Self and be purely logical. Nothing could exhibit this more clearly than Fichte's enunciation of the first principles of the Science of Knowledge. His starting-point is the Ego, which is pure activity. The Ego posits itself. This is the thesis. The antithesis follows; *Within the Ego*, the Ego posits the Non-ego. Thus the distinction between Self and Other falls wholly within the unity of the Self. The reason is that the pure act which is the Ego is an act of thought. What Fichte achieves is the formal description of a dream-experience in which I appear to myself as one element in my own dream.

We must notice, in the second place, another aspect of the experience of resistance. The resistance of the Other is not merely a negation of the act of the Self, it is necessary to the possibility of the act, and so constitutive of it. For without a resistance no action is possible. To act at all is to act *upon something*. Consequently, the Other is discovered in tactual perception both as the resistance to, and the support of action. If I lean with all my weight against a door that has jammed, and it suddenly flies open, I find that the resistance which I was trying to overcome was the support of my effort to overcome it. Without it I lose control of my action and fall headlong. This ambiguity of the Other, as that which sustains all action by resisting it, we must put up with for the time being. For we are committed, in this first volume, to maintaining an ego-centric standpoint, which will only be overcome when, in the second, we consider the mutualities of personal relation.

We must distinguish the perception of resistance from tactual discrimination. The latter is a theoretical activity, aiming to discover something about the object, not to do something to it. When I discover the wall in the dark as an obstacle, I may feel my way along it in the hope of finding an opening, so that I may continue my progress. This is a theoretical activity which forms an essential part of the accomplishment of a practical activity. Tactual discrimination, however, may also be part of a purely theoretical activity, that is to say, of an activity which is undertaken for the sake of knowledge, and determined by no practical intention. But whatever the mode of its relation to action, it is always active; it is discrimination through action. I can discover nothing about the object tactually except by physical movement, and what is so discovered is, in its immediacy, variations of resistance, correlated with variations in movement. The tactual perception of shape, size, weight, hardness, surface texture all depend upon the varying of resistance from zero to a maximum which is determined by the amount of energy which I can bring to bear. But such discrimination involves the co-operation of other forms of sensory awareness; in particular, the kinaesthetic awareness of the movement of my body. The concepts connected directly with tactual discrimination are those which form the basic concepts for the physicist in his description of the material world—energy and momentum, inertia, direction and mass. It would seem therefore that physics is concerned with the translation of an apprehension of the world which is largely visual into terms of tactual experience.

Tactual perception is our only means of having a direct and immediate awareness of the Other as existent. Visual experience does not provide this. For vision is not essentially active; it is characteristically passive. In consequence, visual perception of existent objects is indirect and mediate. Not all visual experience is perceptual. It requires light as its medium of perception; though we can have visual experience without light in the form of visual images. But even when we are looking at a sunlit landscape, a distinction has to be drawn between things and images. Reflections and shadows have to be distinguished from the objects which cast them, and denied an independent reality; yet as objects of vision, as visual sense-data, there is no such distinction. Thus the perception of objects by sight, however psychologically immediate, is logically mediated. It involves essentially a distinction between appearance and reality. It involves the reference of a sense-datum to an existent which is not visually determined.

The significance of this only appears when we consider visual perception from the standpoint of action. For vision, in spite of its negative relation to action, functions primarily in action and as a guide to action. From a theoretical standpoint vision is perception at a distance; but from the practical point of view the spatial must give place to a temporal definition. It is anticipatory perception. It enables us to anticipate contact, that is to say, the resistance of the other; and the distance at which an object is seen is a measure of the time it will take to make contact with it; and so of the movement that must be made before the object can be acted upon. Visual perception is therefore *symbolic*. The sense-datum is a present experience which represents and refers to a future experience of a tactual order in which alone the Other is given. It must therefore be referred to the Self which has the experience, as characterizing him, since it has no objective existence in its own right. In other words, all visual experience is the formation of an image in the Self: it becomes perceptual by being correctly referred to a future tactual perception in which alone an Other-than-self is apprehended. To perceive by sight is to correlate the occurrence of visual imagery with tactual experience, and the capacity to do so has to be learned. Thus the traditional view that images are derived from percepts is, so far as vision at least is concerned, the reverse of the truth. The capacity to form images is a prior condition of the possibility of visual perception.

That all visual experience is imagery is familiar doctrine, though it is usually stated in more general terms. For the assumption that visual experience is the model for all sensory experience leads directly to the generalization that all sensory experience is in its immediacy, subjective, and that it becomes objective through a judgement which refers it beyond itself. Idealism holds this explicitly, realism implicitly and ambiguously. For the realist maintains that what is given in immediate sense-experience is a sense-datum, not a physical object; and the 'existence' of a sense-datum is a Pickwickian existence. The colour of an object exists just as its shadow exists, not in its own right but as a character or property of the existent object. If there is no such object—in a case of hallucination, for example —then the colour that is seen is illusory. More important as evidence, however, is the systematic illusion of perspective which is constitutive for visual perception, and not accidental; and also the abrupt transformations of the visual field when the direction of vision is changed. At least these are difficulties for any theory of vision which treats it from the point of view of the Self as subject. From the point of view of action they are essential to the practical function of sight, the anticipation of contact. In tactual perception there are, strictly speaking, no illusions. What are often described as such are illusions of feeling; and indeed it is misleading even to talk of tactual sense-data. Tactual perception is always perception in action. If we abstract from the action, we no longer have a perceptual element, but a feeling, that is, an element in the general coenasthesia which is the awareness of our own internal state. A prick, for instance, in its immediacy is a feeling of pain which is located in my skin. On the basis of past experience, I may assume an external cause for it; and on occasion I may be wrong. But in any case I do not refer the pricking feeling to the object which causes it, as I do, for example, with a visual sense-datum.

All visual experience, I have said, is the production of an image. Visual *perception* is the reference of an image to the Other. I ought perhaps to justify this generalization of the term 'image', since it may seem to blur the accepted distinction between image and percept, and so deprive us of the distinction between seeing and imagining. My excuse would be that the first step to be taken is precisely to abolish this distinction in its traditional form. We can then distinguish, when necessary, different classes of images. The common usage of language does this. A graven image is a physical object; an image in a mirror is still perceived, not imagined. Only a 'mental' image is not perceived but *merely* imagined. Since we have rejected the dualism of mind and matter, the philosophical distinction between mental and bodily seeing, between image and percept, is no longer valid for us, and what basis there is for it requires reformulation. From the standpoint of the Agent cognition is included in action, as the negative aspect of action, without which action would not be action but merely happening there would be no acts but only events. We might therefore distinguish, as a first approximation, between images which are, and images which are not referred to the immediate field of action. Now in action the function of visual perception is anticipatory. Consequently the reference of the visual image is its location in space. The components of this location are direction and distance from the position of the Agent. We must therefore distinguish between images which are rightly located and images which are not. The latter are illusory anticipations of contact. It is this difference to which we often refer when we talk of seeing the image of a thing and not the thing itself, or more generally when we distinguish, in visual experience, between appearance and reality. Consider three cases of visual imagery; the image formed when we look at an object; when we look at its reflection in a mirror; and when we reproduce the image with closed eyes. Let us assume a perfect mirror and an observer with perfect visualizing powers. Then these three images, *quâ* images, are not merely similar, but identical. We call the mirror reflection a mirror-image, or a mere appearance, or an illusory perception because it is wrongly located; that is, because if we go in the direction and to the distance at which we locate it, we shall not find ourselves in contact with the object. Yet if we look at the object through a periscope, we see the thing itself, and not an 'image' of it, because the visual location of the object, both as to direction and distance, is practically correct, in spite of the double reflection. Even the 'illusion' of the single mirror image disappears with practical experience, and the driver of a car sees another vehicle approaching from behind by looking at his driving mirror. In the same way the systematic 'illusions' of perspective are essential to the functioning of visual perception, since they provide the basis for the correct location of the image in depth. Here the mediacy of visual perception is particularly obvious, because our apprehension of distance varies so remarkably with changes in atmospheric and other conditions. The capacity to correlate visual with tactual experience has to be learned.

We need not carry this issue farther. It will serve our purpose better if we consider, from the new standpoint, the phenomena of consciousness in general. The term 'consciousness' has followed the term 'experience' into the outer darkness to which philosophy banishes words that will not behave themselves. The reason for this is the trouble produced by the dualism inherent in a purely theoretical standpoint. It is time to reinstate them when dualism is overcome. 'Experience' is a practical concept, referring to whatever is apprehended in action, in distinction from what is thought in reflection. 'Consciousness' on the other hand is a general term for all sub-rational awareness, which may be conceived either as all that remains when we abstract from the rationality of our own awareness, or as an actual form of awareness in sub-rational creatures, or in rational beings under abnormal conditions. 'Rational consciousness' means 'knowledge'. It is a legitimate term only because knowledge, being personal, contains, and is constituted by, its own negation. Since knowledge is the negative aspect of action, and action may in consequence be termed 'rational behaviour', 'consciousness' is properly 'conscious behaviour' and as such it is a term which serves to isolate the subject matter of empirical psychology.

We are faced at the outset with a methodological problem. How can we determine theoretically, and so represent conceptually, the other's consciousness, whether the other be another human being or an animal? From the standpoint of the 'Cogito', with its dualism of mind and matter, the answer is that we cannot. This is indeed the reason why all philosophy which adopts this standpoint reduces logically to solipsism, and so refutes itself. But from the standpoint of the 'I do' consciousness is the negative aspect of conscious behaviour; that is, of a form of behaviour which necessitates consciousness as a ground of its possibility. We know that a cat sees, because we see it using its eyes to anticipate contact; just as we know that a man, with eyes like our own, is blind, through observing his failures to anticipate contact by using his eyes. If it is asked how we know that this involves the cat in forming a visual image, the answer is is that to anticipate a future contact necessitates a present symbol, and if it is visual then the symbol is a visual image. If we are asked how we know that the image the cat forms is identical with the one we form when we see the same object, the answer is that we do not. So far as the cat's eye is constructed like our own it is reasonable to assume this; if there are differences of construction it is reasonable to assume a difference in the image.

We know that colour-blind people do not form the same images as we do. We know also that they see, and that they form visual images of some sort. We know that they are visually conscious.

There is therefore no difficulty, arising from our inability to see through any eyes other than our own, to be overcome. To think that there is would be like thinking that we cannot understand what someone says to us, without knowing whether he uses visual or auditory or no imagery at all in thinking it. What does require to be pointed out in this connexion is something different. The common notion that there is no difficulty in knowing how inorganic bodies move, or no special difficulty; that the special difficulty arises when we try to understand the behaviour of conscious organisms, is the opposite of the truth. Formally and theoretically there is no special difficulty at all; our knowledge of the Other, whatever the Other may be, is of the same kind. But in practice we understand any form of behaviour better the closer it is to our own.

All human knowledge is necessarily anthropomorphic, for the simple reason that we are human beings. By this I mean that we can only determine the behaviour of the Other through a knowledge of our own. We have already noted that tactual perception distinguishes immediately between Self and Other. Yet in itself, as mere experience of resistance, it *determines* neither. It depends, as we have seen, upon the 'I do' which accompanies all my activity. There is however no corresponding 'The Other does' which is immediately given. For this reason my knowledge of myself has a priority over my knowledge of the Other. I can understand the Other only by imputing to it a determination of the Self. The Other is given as a resistance to my action; I must therefore characterize the Other as an agent like myself, acting against me. In general, then, the rule for the determination of the activity of the Other is this: I must attribute to the Other, if I am to understand it, the form of activity that I attribute to myself. My understanding of the behaviour of the Other is always mediated through my understanding of my own. For I have an immediate awareness of my own states and activities and their modifications which I do not have of those of the Other.

This inevitable anthropomorphism is undoubtedly the reason for the animism both of young children and of primitive Man. It may also provide the justification of religious belief. But at this point in the argument we are in no position to say so. The anthropomorphism of which I speak is not necessarily animistic; and it characterizes physical science just as much as religion. We do not necessarily characterize every particular other, by crediting it with *all* the characteristics of the Self, particularly with its rational characteristics. Our knowledge is anthropomorphic in the sense that whatever characteristics we attribute to the Other must be included within the full characterization of ourselves. When we distinguish between persons and material things, the characteristics we attribute to things are a selection from the characteristics we attribute to a person. All the characteristics of a material object are also characteristics of a person. He *is* a material object, though that is not a complete nor a sufficient characterization. When I say then that our knowledge of the physical world, however scientific, is anthropomorphic, I mean that unless I had fallen downstairs, or otherwise lost control of my movements, I could not understand what was meant by 'a body falling freely through space'. We can state this generally. The concept of 'a person' is inclusive of the concept of 'an organism', as the concept of 'an organism' is inclusive of that of 'a material body'. The included concepts can be derived from the concept of 'a person' by abstractions; by excluding from attention those characters which belong to the higher category alone. The empirical ground for these distinctions is found in practical experience. We cannot deal with organisms successfully in the same way that we can with material objects, or with persons. The form of their resistance— in opposition or in support—necessitates a difference in our own behaviour. The empirical genesis of the 'mind' and 'matter' dualism lies in this, that having abstracted the concept of a 'material' object from the concept of a 'person' in this way, we then illegitimately form a concept, on the negative analogy of 'the material' by thinking a unity of what has been excluded. This is the concept of the 'non-material' or 'the mind', or of 'consciousness' as an independently existing entity.

Before distinguishing different levels of consciousness, we must rid ourselves of the effects, in the psychological field, of this dualistic construction. It appears as a hypothesis of psycho-physical parallelism. Now there are abnormal experiences for which this is a not inappropriate description. If I fall from a height into the sea, I lose control completely of the movement of my body. I cannot act. Yet I am conscious of falling. We might reasonably say in such a case that my consciousness accompanies, or runs parallel with, the movement of my body, without affecting it. But in this precisely consists the abnor-mality of the experience. Normal experience presents a strong contrast with this, since then my consciousness is one of the determinants of my bodily movement. There can be no possible doubt of this. If I lose consciousness while walking I fall down. Not only does what I am doing stop, but the form of my observable behaviour alters to that of a material body. Now any factor in a movement the exclusion of which alters the form of the movement is *ipso facto* a determinant of the movement. When I act, therefore, my consciousness—my seeing, hearing, remembering, thinking—does not *accompany* but is *integrated with* my bodily movements and is a part-determinant of them. The body-mind problem is therefore fictitious. That it exists merely proves that there is an error in our representation of mind or of body or of both. It is, however, desirable not to use the term 'cause' in this connexion. For though causality used to have, and still sometimes has a significance which covers all types of determination, it is now more familiar in a narrower usage which applies only to the determination of physical movement by other physical movements. Even the behaviour of plants is better described in terms of reaction to stimulus than in terms of cause and effect.

'Conscious behaviour' then, is an abstraction from 'action'. The abstraction consists in excluding rationality from the concept of action. The term 'behaviour' is strictly an organic concept. Inorganic entities do not behave, they merely move. We have good reason to believe that some organisms behave consciously while others do not; but in either case we seek to understand behaviour by considering the movement of an organism as a reaction to stimulus; while we understand inorganic movement as the effect of a cause, and action as the realization of an intention. We seek the *reason* for an action. Thus in seeking to understand human behaviour the psychologist considers it from the organic point of view, as reaction to stimulus. He is right in this, since the abstraction from rationality is the principle which delimits his field of inquiry, and human beings, whatever more they may be, are organisms. This means of course that psychology cannot give a complete account of human behaviour, and if, in particular cases, the account is complete, then the behaviour in question is abnormal; that is, it is actually, and not merely theoretically dissociated from any rational determination.

These remarks may enable us to understand the assertion which I now proceed to make. Consciousness is primarily motive, not cognitive. Whether it is ever cognitive depends on how we define cognition. If by cognition we mean knowledge, then consciousness is never cognitive, since knowledge depends upon the awareness of a distinction between Self and Other, and this is the basis of rational (or irrational) behaviour. We need not settle this issue, which must be left to the psychologists; we may proceed instead to explain and exemplify what is meant by 'motive consciousness'. Let us suppose that we were trying to construct a purely hypothetical account of the evolution of consciousness. We could proceed only by distinguishing a hierarchy of levels within our own human consciousness, such that though each level is a conceivably viable form of consciousness by itself, every higher level is viable only if it includes the levels below it. Our first question might be this, 'What is the lower limit of consciousness?' The obvious answer would be that it must consist in a bare capacity to distinguish between comfort and discomfort, which is the lowest form of pleasure-pain discrimination. Below this consciousness disappears, and we are left with an organism which reacts to stimulus without consciousness. At this point we find that the terms we use become ambiguous. They sometimes do and sometimes do not imply the presence of consciousness. Such terms as 'sensitiveness', 'attraction' and 'repulsion', are applied to magnets and to plants; yet they are also used to indicate modes of consciousness. This indicates simply that around the lower limit of consciousness we are not sure, in a particular case, whether the reaction to stimulus we observe is a conscious reaction or entirely non-conscious.

What concerns us is that consciousness emerges as a new element in the determination of an organism's reaction to stimulus. It makes possible a form of behaviour which would not be possible in its absence. For our present purpose we need only notice a few points of interest. First, the reason for distinguishing between 'cause-effect' and 'stimulus-reaction' is that the former is included in the latter. If I tread on the cat's tail, the effect that I cause is the crushing of the tissues of the tail by the weight of my body. This occasions a feeling of pain in the cat. But the reaction of the cat to the stimulus is with voice and teeth and claws. A reaction could of course occur as the behaviour of an organism without consciousness of any kind; but if pain is occasioned then the pain is an element in the determination of the reaction. In fact, the concept of reaction to stimulus is teleological, whether consciousness is present or no. To use it is to imply that the movements in question cannot be fully *described* without reference to an end. Teleological language, in this—which is the Aristotelian—sense is descriptive, not explanatory. Aristotle, we may remember, found it adequate to the description of the growth of plants; but not, without modification, to the description of human action, because of the presence of an image of the end.

Secondly, consciousness at this level is purely *motive*. It is occasioned by a stimulus from the environment, and is a factor in determining the reaction which, if successful, is an adaptation of the organism to the environment. It is an awareness, but not an awareness of anything; not of the stimulus nor of the reaction nor of the environment. If we call all modes of consciousness of this type 'feeling', then we can say that all feeling is motive consciousness, and is in no sense cognitive. It is the manner in which an organism is affected by a stimulus. A feeling of pain is simply a painful feeling; and since it is the organism that is 'affected', the feeling is a self-awareness which is not an awareness of self. In relation to the environmental stimulus, which is not cognized, feeling is an element in the reaction, the rest of the reaction being a movement of the organism in relation to its environment, which may, on occasion, be a suppression of movement. The feeling is integrated with the movement; so we may describe it as a 'moving-feeling' which is not a feeling of movement, which would imply a distinguishing of the movement from the feeling. Within the total reaction the feeling functions as the directing or selective element. It selects the direction of the movement, without being an awareness of selection. It makes a variation of movement in reaction possible which would not occur without it. It raises the level of reaction from 'mere movement' to 'conscious movement'.

Thirdly: a reaction which is below this level is 'unconscious'. It is, however, still a reaction to stimulus, and so an adaptation to the environment. It requires teleological description. We must therefore presuppose an unconscious '*rapport*' between organism and environment, which unites them in a practical organic reciprocity. This cannot be a purely causal relation, since it involves the use of teleological terms—such as 'function' and 'adaptation'— to describe it. In this sense all consciousness presupposes an 'unconscious', which is not a mere negation of consciousness, but a negative element within it. Since 'consciousness' is an abstraction—a limitation of attention to an element in a reaction which cannot exist by itself,—the full statement should be that conscious adaptation to environment pre-supposes unconscious adaptation.

Fourthly, this primary level of conscious behaviour permits of a considerable degree of discrimination within its conscious element, which is itself correlated with a range of variation in the reaction to stimulus. The primary formal distinction is between positive and negative feeling, which direct movements of attraction and movements of repulsion respectively. There is evidence that negative is prior to positive feeling, so that the lowest limit of consciousness is a feeling integrated with a defensive reaction. In our own consciousness, it is discriminated as 'fear' and is the correlate of the recognition of danger. The positive feelings would then be developed within behaviour by contrast, as integrated with and directing movements of positive adaptation. Defence reactions designate the environment as opposing, and positive reactions as supporting the life of the organism. As a result, consciousness in general is primarily negative, and its positive aspects are derivative. The qualitative discriminations of feeling we need not consider in this context.

What does concern us particularly is the distinction between this level of consciousness and a higher one, which is character-ized by the development of special senses. Since our purpose is not psychological but philosophical we may limit our attention to the critical case, which is that of vision. Our question is whether the special senses, which belong to a higher level of consciousness, differ from feeling in being cognitive rather than motive, and if so, in what sense. Vision has clearly the highest claim to be in itself cognitive, and is therefore sufficient for our purpose. But something must first be said about tactual experi-ence, if only because we have already assigned it the primacy in cognition as the awareness of the Other.

All sensory awareness is a phenomenon of contact between organism and environment. If we ignore, for our purpose, internal stimuli as a special case, we may say that this contact takes place at the surface of the organism. Something touches the organism in all awareness, but all awareness is not therefore tactual experience. Touch, therefore, as a special sense, is the awareness of contact and therefore of the distinction between Self and Other, and all cognition by means of touch is a tactual discrimination which presupposes this. Below this level, the awareness produced by contact is a *feeling*, and such awareness is purely motive. We must beware, in this context, of relying on the physiology of the nervous system as a guide. There are special nerves for pain, but not for pleasure, but pain and pleasure are both feelings. Touch, therefore, as a special sense, is above the level of subjective consciousness; it is the lower limit of a consciousness of objects.

Vision differs from feeling in that it requires a capacity to produce images. Whereas a feeling of pain is a painful feeling, seeing a blue circle is not a circular blue seeing. It is a presentation. But this does not mean that the image is apprehended as an image, in distinction from a percept. Nor does it mean that the organism distinguishes between its seeing and what it sees. The reason for the ambiguity of the term 'sensation' is that at the level of sensory consciousness there is no distinction between the sensing and what is sensed. What takes its place is the distinction between feeling and sensing. For sense presupposes feeling and is necessarily accompanied by it, even if the feeling is not attended to. Feeling is the primary mode in which we are affected by objects, and forms the matrix of consciousness within which presentational consciousness is occasioned. That sense is derivative from feeling can, I believe, be shown, though I do not wish to spend time now in submitting the evidence. I shall mention one point in it only. The stimulation of a special sense provides, up to a certain maximum of intensity, a clearer presentation; beyond this maximum only a feeling of pain. If the stimulus is decreased sufficiently we reach a point where we 'feel', rather than 'sense' something. It is, we say, 'as if' there were an image though actually there is not. The simplest explanation of this seems to be that a feeling is present which would generate an image if the stimulus were a little stronger; and the character of the feeling, as a result of experience, enables us to anticipate the image, and so functions, in the control of behaviour, as the image would if it were formed. This may be the basis of what is described as 'imageless thinking'.

To our main question, whether the formation of an image is cognitive, the answer must be a negative one. Sense, like feeling, is, in itself, purely motive. It is a mode of awareness which enormously increases the possibility of discrimination in the reaction to a stimulus. The range of discrimination in feeling is considerable; but it is very small relatively to the possible discriminations in a visual field. Indeed the possibilities of visual discrimination far exceed the possibilities of muscular discrimination in behaviour. There is an overplus of refinement in visual discrimination beyond what is necessary for the guidance of the most sensitive reaction, and in which the organism can take pleasure without being able to employ it practically. This may even result in a kind of reflective activity which has no practical reference; and it is the probable source of dreaming, certainly of the immense preponderance of visual elements in dreaming.

Even at its most primitive, visual experience is spatial, and the intuition of space is primarily visual. We may imagine the most primitive form of vision as a mere capacity to distinguish light and dark. Perhaps the most primitive form of visual organ enables its possessor only to 'see sparks' when danger approaches, and this experience may activate a defence reaction. Perhaps this primitive vision is what we see when we are in the dark—a vague pattern of light and shade, or 'spots before the eyes'. Such vision is clearly not cognitive, but motive. Its matrix, we may suppose, would be a feeling of fear, or something analogous to fear; and as a secondary derivative could produce a feeling of security directing movements of attraction. From that first glimmering of sight to the complicated discriminations of our own visual experience is a very long process of development, but it contains nothing new in principle, until we reach the point at which the distinction between Self and Other is made. Up to that point visual awareness remains, like feeling, purely motive. There is no cognition. In this respect sensory experience, like feeling, is below the level of knowledge. The highest reach of this level of consciousness we might describe as 'dream' consciousness. For a dream is a highly discriminated form of consciousness which is not cognitive, but merely a reaction to a stimulus. I may dream that I am on a polar expedition and wake to find that it is freezing and the blankets have fallen off the bed. The dream is a reaction to the stimulus; my waking experience is a *cognition* of the same stimulus. The difference between the two is the difference between motive and cognitive consciousness, or between an organic and a personal consciousness; and the personal consciousness, in virtue of its form, contains the organic consciousness, as its negative element, within itself.

Below the level of the personal, then, there is no cognition, since knowledge, in any sense of the term, presupposes the 'I do': there is no action, but only reaction to stimulus. The functional difference between feeling and sense is that sense enables the reaction to *anticipate* contact, and this is especially true of visual consciousness. By substituting, as stimulus, light reflected from an object for actual contact with the object, it makes possible an anticipatory adaptation on the part of the organism, without any cognition of the object.

We may conclude this aspect of our subject with three reflections. Firstly, an account of consciousness, defined as we have defined it, is necessarily behaviouristic. But a behaviouristic psychology is under no need to deny consciousness. The tendency to do so comes from presupposing the mind-matter dualism, and endeavouring to get rid of the difficulties which result by suppressing one of the correlates. A behaviourism which does deny consciousness is self-refuting. It proposes to describe organic behaviour by excluding all elements which cannot be observed or inferred from observation. But 'observing' and 'inferring' cannot be observed; and no theory, not even a behaviourist theory, is then possible.

Secondly, there is no way, in theory, from an organic consciousness to a personal consciousness involving knowledge and action. No development of motive consciousness can ever amount to cognitive consciousness. The reason for this is that the concept of organic consciousness is constituted by abstraction from personal consciousness, by eliminating the personal element of action and knowledge. The only way to reach a personal consciousness, therefore, is by deliberately passing beyond the limits of our isolate and reintroducing the elements which were excluded. A more inclusive concept cannot be derived from a less inclusive. The organic idea can be derived from the personal, but the process cannot be reversed.

Finally, since at the organic level sensory experience is no more cognitive than feeling, there is no *a priori* reason—and as we shall see later, no empirical reason—why at the personal level, feeling should not be as much an element in cognition as sense. For it is a person who knows in acting, not his mind or his thought, and feeling, like sense, is a necessary element in any personal consciousness. The psychological analysis of consciousness into cognitive, affective and conative aspects is misleading even when a faculty psychology is repudiated and the unity of consciousness is stressed. It is itself the lingering ghost of the faculty psychology, and it is high time that it was laid. Consciousness, as such, has no cognitive element. Only persons know, in any proper sense of the term, and act with knowledge. And they know, and develop their knowledge, as much through their capacity for feeling as by using their senses; perhaps even more so, since sense depends upon feeling in a manner in which feeling does not depend upon sense.

CHAPTER SIX

Implications of Action

We must now consider some of the most general implications of action, and, in particular, some of the very general modifications which have to be made in traditional philosophical theory when we adopt the standpoint of the Agent rather than of the Thinker. In doing this we shall be laying the foundations for a theory of action, not primarily for a theory of knowledge; yet such a theory of action will exhibit the form of the personal by including within it, as its negative aspect, a theory of knowledge.

Since the 'I do' which is the absolute presupposition of all our experience, contains the 'I know that I do' as a constitutive aspect of itself, we can lay down at once a negative criterion for the truth of any philosophical theory. The 'I do' is indubitable. It is presupposed in the act of denying it: its contradictory is, therefore, self-contradictory. It follows from this that any theory which either explicitly or by implication denies the 'I do', that is to say, denies that there is action, is false. This negative principle has a very wide range of application. It disposes at once of any theory that implies that the world is fully determinate; for to assert this is precisely to deny the possibility of action, though not of course, the possibility of activity. The 'I do' is not problematic.

We may go further than this; for it is an immediate corollary that whatever is necessarily implied in the possibility of action is itself certain. We have already seen that the possibility of knowledge is so implied; and consequently the possibility of knowledge is not problematic. Any purely sceptical theory is therefore false. Our immediate business is to bring to light some of those necessary implications which have their guarantee in the fact that there is action.

We may begin by defining action itself—not its mere logical form, but the form of its actuality—as a unity of movement and knowledge. Some comments are necessary to elucidate the definition and to prevent misunderstanding. In the first place the notion of *unity* must be taken strictly. Movement and knowledge are inseparable aspects of all action, not separable elements in a complex. To represent action as consisting of a cognition which is the *cause* of a movement is to misrepresent the unity of action radically. We relapse into the mind-matter dualism if we analyse an action into two events, the one subjective and the other objective, which stand in causal relation. This is not merely untrue to experience; it is a logical monstrosity. That thought moves nothing is an implicate of the concept of thought. An act may indeed be analysed into a number of elements which compose it, but each of these elements is itself an act, and itself therefore a unity of knowledge and movement. What is distinguishable theoretically is not necessarily separable in fact: for to distinguish elements in a whole theoretically is merely to limit attention to an aspect of what is presented. In order therefore to eliminate this tendency to misunderstand the definition I propose to call knowledge and movement *dimensions* of action. The use of the metaphor is intended only to keep before our minds the indivisible unity of knowledge and movement in action.

In the second place the terms movement and knowledge must not be construed objectively. By 'movement' is not meant an observed displacement in space; nor by 'knowledge' an ascertained truth. The two terms represent, on the contrary, a theoretical analysis of the 'I do' into 'I move' and 'I know'. 'Movement' here refers to our experience of moving ourselves; 'knowledge' to the awareness of the Other which 'informs' this moving. We might rephrase it thus: 'When there is an acting there is a moving and a knowing, and the indivisible unity of these constitutes the acting.' I make no apologies for using the term 'knowledge' in this connexion. It is the proper term to use; for this is its primary significance, from which other usages are derived by qualification. Knowledge is that in my action which makes it an action and not a blind activity. It is 'objective' awareness; or rather awareness of the Other and the Self in relation. It is not 'knowing that', neither is it 'knowing how'; neither is it 'knowledge by acquaintance', for it *is* acquaintance. We use the term 'know' in this primary sense when we say that we know our friends and are known by them. If it is objected that knowing implies certainty and that the term should only be used, at least in a philosophical context, to express certainty, I reply that this is what we are doing, though why anything less than certainty—the whole of science, for instance—should be excluded from knowledge I cannot understand. All *reflective* judgements are hypothetical and have an element of logical uncertainty in them; but if I say that I know someone I cannot be mistaken. If the statement is false then I am lying.

Thirdly, we must remember that all personal activities have the form of a positive which includes its negative. This is the form of the unity of movement and knowledge in action. Knowledge is the negative which constitutes action by its inclusion in movement—which is the positive dimension. But if we distinguish the two dimensions, each of them has the same form. Moving includes its own negative—not, of course, rest as mere absence of movement, but a negative activity, a resistance to movement. If it did not, I could not move, I should simply fall down. The active resistance to movement is a condition of the possibility of my moving. We may borrow here from science the distinction between 'kinetic' and 'potential' energy, which indeed is derived from the personal experience of moving, by abstracting from its personal completeness. The experience 'I do' is an experience of expending energy. In its positive mode, as 'I act', this expenditure of energy expresses itself positively in a bodily movement. In its negative mode, as 'I think' the energy is still expended, but it is self-negated; I my-self provide a resistance to the tendency of cognition to 'pass over' into action, which negates the tendency, so that the energy remains 'potential'. That thinking does involve an expenditure of energy is shown by the fact that it can produce bodily fatigue.

Knowledge in action is similarly constituted by its own negative. Knowing in action is possible only through an active ignoring of most of what is presented, that is to say, by a selectivity of attention. I can only ignore what I am aware of, and the elements in the situation are apprehended. So we find ourselves saying at times that we were 'unconsciously' aware of a thing when our attention was concentrated on something else. These unnoticed elements in the situation however play an essential role in the determination of our action. We see them and respond to them, without noticing them. Now we have already contrasted cognition with motive consciousness in an earlier chapter.[1] We now see that knowledge[2]—which is cognitive consciousness—depends for its possibility upon the inclusion within it of a non-cognitive or motive consciousness. This indeed is the basis of habit; and habit is a necessary constituent of any actual action. Habit is conscious behaviour, or response to stimulus which involves awareness. But in human behaviour, save in abnormal conditions such as somnambulism, it can only be present as a negative element in action. This organic consciousness is, then, the negative aspect in the constitution of personal consciousness.

Since we are considering the Self as agent, and therefore in its existence, and from the standpoint of action, we are not required, like Kant, to adopt purely theoretical procedures. We must of course proceed by abstraction if we are to consider the universal character of action; but the abstraction is a practical one, by which I mean a limitation of attention to the most

[1] Chapter V, pp. 119 ff.
[2] 'Knowledge' here refers to primary knowledge or knowledge in action; not to secondary or reflective knowledge.

general characters of something that is itself actual, and not merely theoretical. I propose therefore to follow the method employed by Sir Isaac Newton in determining the principles of motion, and to consider the Agent as a particle in space and time, at an infinite distance from all other particles. We shall have to endow this particle with the power of movement and the power to know itself and its environment. This is a legitimate procedure, since we merely restore the complete situation from which Newton's moving particle is abstracted by ignoring the element of consciousness. The advantage to be gained is that we eliminate from attention the complex influence of the Other upon the action of the Self, while still considering the Self as an existent. We exclude also the complexity of internal conditions which necessarily determine any particular act. We consider the Agent simply in respect of his agency, alone in an undifferentiated environment. The capacity to act is then represented by the capacity to move; and the suppression of all differentiation in the environment reduces it to empty space and time. We are imagining, *per impossibile*, an action which requires neither support nor resistance, just as Newton does.

What we cannot eliminate, if we are to think movement at all, is space and time; and our first question must be about the nature of these. If the agent moves, he must move from 'here-now' to 'there-then' and a spatio-temporal determination is involved. If we objectify the movement, by eliminating the activity of moving, so that the movement is merely contemplated by a subject, we find we can eliminate the reference to time, and say simply the agent moves from 'here' to 'there'. This however describes a 'possible' moving only. If the moving is actual, the time factor must come in. Space would seem then to represent the *possibility* of movement rather than its *actuality*; and this is confirmed by the observation that in an actual movement the space factor is one-dimensional. The other dimensions of space represent merely paths that the movement did *not* take, or possible paths that it might have taken. We might almost say that the space-factor is simply the time-factor objectified, or

thought, either in anticipation or in retrospect. For in retrospect all the successiveness in the actual movement disappears,
and all its moments are apprehended simultaneously. From the
point of view of the Subject, therefore, time is spatialized, and
is represented by a 'line', or 'path' or 'track'. We can only
distinguish space from time by saying that in space all the
elements are simultaneous; not, as in time, successive; and
simultaneity is itself a determination of time. This indicates that
time is logically prior to space; and if we remember that all
reflection is included in action as its negative component, the
relativity of space and time is accounted for, since the reflective discrimination of space from time must be relative to the
action of moving. We can put this in another way. From the
standpoint of action, the distance of an object from the present
position of an agent is a representation of the time that must
elapse before he can come into contact with it; and this time is
relative to the velocity of his movement.

This logical priority of time is clearly recognized if we recall
the distinction between positive and negative activity. The
negative mode of 'doing' is, we have said, 'thinking'. Thinking
does not involve an actual movement, but only a permanent
tendency to pass over into movement which is continuously
negated. It has therefore no spatial factor, but only a temporal
one. The 'I do' is necessarily temporal, for all doing takes time.
But the 'I think' in its actuality is *only* temporal. Space remains
merely virtual, as the possibility of realizing what is thought in
a practical activity.

We are now in a position to summarize these considerations
by asserting that time is the form of action; while space is the
form of reflection, and that time is prior to space because
action is prior to reflection. The priority is that of the positive
in respect of the negative which it includes. That time and
space are mere forms, and in themselves nothing, needs no
argument. They are negations of intuition; ideal lower limits of
imaginal consciousness. To see an empty space between two
objects, is to apprehend the possibility of moving between them

without resistance. We ought to note here, however, that it may be misleading to ground our account of space upon visual experience. A man born blind is as much involved in the determination of space as any other, and his mode of apprehending space is open also to those whose sight is unimpaired. The tactual awareness of space is more fundamental than the visual; the latter being, as we have seen, a mediate apprehension which refers to the immediacy of touch. If we disregard vision, space reveals itself much more evidently as a tactually apprehended possibility of movement; as the absence of a resistance anticipated as possible.

Since time is the positive and space the negative form, we must begin with time; and consider it from the standpoint of the Agent. Time, we have said, is the form of action. If the agent moves, he is aware of his moving and of time as the form of his motion. And since he is aware of the motion as his doing, he is aware of time as the form generated by his doing, whether as positive doing (movement) or negative doing (thought). In consequence, time cannot be apprehended directly in reflection. It can only be represented symbolically, and the primary symbol is spatial. Time, and indeed action, of which it is the form, cannot be object for a subject. It can only be experienced in action. In such experience of time, the characteristic structure is a distinction between past and future. When the agent moves his action continues. At any point in this continuing movement he is aware of the distinction between past and future. The past is what has been done; the future what has not been done but remains to do. That part of the movement which is past is already actual, the part which is future is not actual but only possible. In general, therefore, the past is the field of actuality, the future the field of possibility. The present is simply the point of action. Now to be actual is to exist; consequently the past is that which exists, and the future that which does not exist. It is not that which will exist, for the action may not be completed, or it may complete itself in an unanticipated manner; and in any case the future never comes. When what is now future comes to existence, it is no longer future but past.

In action, then, the Agent generates a past by actualizing a possibility. This 'generation', or 'bringing into existence', is practical determination, and the actual is the determinate. To act, therefore, is to determine; and the Agent is the determiner. To determine is to make actual what is, apart from the acting, merely possible. Theoretical determination is the negative of this, and is contained within it as the specific awareness of what has been practically determined by the agent. We may therefore define acting as determining the future. The past is then that which has been determined, and is, in consequence, completely determinate.

This analysis has certain important implications. The first concerns the conception traditionally termed 'free-will', and its negation, 'determinism'. To possess free-will is simply to be able to determine the indeterminate, that is, the future. We can now see that this is implied in the very conception of action. The Agent is the determiner. To deny free-will is to deny the possibility of action. We have already established, as a negative criterion of truth, that any theory which denies the possibility of action is false. That I am free is an immediate implication of the 'I do'; and to deny freedom is to assert that no one ever *does* anything, that no one is capable even of thinking or of observing.

What then of the antinomy of freedom? This antinomy arises, we have seen, because knowledge presupposes the determinateness of its object. Only that which is already determinate can be determined reflectively by thought. But the antinomy depends upon the 'I think'. When we insist on the primacy of the practical, and adopt the standpoint of the Agent, rather than of the Subject, the antinomy between freedom and determinism vanishes. Knowledge is necessarily of the actual, or the existent. The merely possible, the non-existent, cannot be known. We have seen that the actual or the existent is the past. It is that which is determinate because it has been already determined. To act is to determine the future: the past is already determinate. Knowledge, then, in its primary form, is the theoretical determination of the past in action. The freedom of the agent then, so far from being incompatible with the possibility of knowledge is the ground of that possibility. The Agent, in action, generates the determinate as the object of knowledge. The falsity of determinism lies simply in the dogma that the future is already determinate. But if this were so there would be no future; the future would be already past.

The qualifications that this statement requires, that is to say, the recognition of the negative which it necessarily includes, will concern us in the sequel. For the moment we are considering the Agent as solitary in empty space and time. In such a situation, if it were possible, the agent could determine the future in any way he pleased. His freedom would be unlimited. What does in fact limit the freedom of particular agents is the presence of other agents in the same field of action. But there is one limitation which arises apart from this, which is indeed a self-limitation of the Agent's freedom by his own action. In determining the future he determines an environment which itself provides a limitation to his further action. This is the principle of the irreversibility of action, and therefore of the form of action, which is time.

But before dealing with the limitation of freedom, we must consider the spatial factor in action more closely. Space, we have asserted, is the form of reflection. By reflection is meant the negative aspect of action, which in contrast with movement we have called knowledge. As a negative *activity* we have identified it with thought, intending by thought a conscious activity which proceeds in terms of a distinction between true and false. As an actual activity of the personal, thought, as a spontaneity of the Self, must include a negative aspect or receptivity, which we call sense-perception. But 'thinking' is an ambiguous term, often restricted to that form of reflective activity which intends knowledge, and so to the processes of inference. There are other forms of reflective activity; that for instance which proceeds in terms of the distinction between beautiful and ugly. Both of these are forms of secondary reflection. The primary reflection is the reflective element in action, which proceeds in terms of the distinction between right and wrong.[1]

When we say then that space is the form of reflection, the primary reference is to knowing in action, to the reflective element in acting, though there is a secondary and mediate reference to activities which are constituted by a reflective intention. The bare form of this awareness is spatial. If we start from the concrete awareness of a world of objects, then all those objects are presented simultaneously, without a temporal discrimination. But they are also represented separately, as occupying different locations, that is different positions relative to the position of the agent. From the agent's point of view these objects represent resistances (and also supports) to his action. Their distances from him represent the time of his movement which must elapse before making contact with them. Their distances from one another represent an empty space through which he can move without resistance from them; their directions, the direction of his movement if he decides to make contact with them. If now we eliminate the objects in imagination what remains is empty space; and from the Agent's point of view this is the awareness of an infinite number of possible directions of movement.

We may realize this in another way by reference to a retrospective rather than an anticipatory awareness. When I move I am also aware of my movement. But this is possible through a distinction between my present position and the positions I have successively occupied before. But I am aware of all the positions I have occupied since the start of my movement simultaneously, as the path I have followed, and this is a spatial determination. I represent the time factor as a path (i.e. a line). This does not mislead me, because my activity of reflection has its own temporal form. I can read the successiveness of my past movement into the line by attending successively to differen-

[1] The terms 'right' and 'wrong' here have no specifically moral connotation.

tiated points upon it. I supply the time factor from my own theoretical activity. I can, of course, take the points in the line in any order I please. I can reverse the order of movement. But so long as it is I who am moving, the continuation of my movement and the position I now occupy, determine the order in which I must take them. It is only when I am being passively moved—at rest in a train, for instance, that I can be in doubt whether it is my train or the train beside it which is moving. Kant, you may remember, offered the reversibility of a movement as a criterion for distinguishing between subjective and objective time. He had to do this because he was thinking from the standpoint of the Subject-self. From the standpoint of the Self as agent the criterion is unnecessary.

We can now return to the irreversibility of action, and to the limitation of freedom which this implies. Consider again the solitary agent in empty space. He can move from here-now to there-then. This movement cannot be repeated. He can of course move from Edinburgh to Glasgow every week. But each repetition is *another* movement, at a later date. The first movement creates a determinate past, and all action is into the future. What has been determined remains for ever determinate; what has been done cannot be undone. Action is irreversible. That time is irreversible is merely the abstract or formal way of stating this. It is an immediate implication of the very form of 'doing', whether active or reflective.

This characterization of space and time as the forms respectively of reflection and of action has important implications. We have to recall now that reflection is only actual as the negative aspect of action, and so as contained within it. We must therefore consider space and time in their unity as the form of action, space being the negative element which is contained within time. Consider first the physicist's conception of the space-time continuum. It follows from what has been said that the time factor in this continuum is not real time, or rather that it is only past time, and consequently it is spatialized. For this reason it has sometimes been described as a 'fourth dimension' of space. Real time is constituted by the distinction between past and future. From a purely theoretical point of view action is excluded, and only reflection remains. To think this we are driven to represent ourselves as pure observers travelling, or rather being carried from the past into the future, and so discovering as we move a future world which was already determinate, though we have only now reached it. Time here is obviously replaced by space, and the movement is represented as a movement of the observer. But it is impossible to think this through without a patent contradiction. It means that the form of the world is a four-dimensional space, and only the observer is in time, and therefore external to the world— whatever this can be made to signify.

Let us put this in a non-metaphorical way. I can imagine myself at any point in space or time—as living, for example, under Pericles in ancient Athens. If I do this, while actually I am in Scotland now, I must think the time that has elapsed since then as future relative to my imaginary existence in the fifth century B.C. But this future is, as I am well aware, already determinate, and some at least of its determinations I know. I think it as future, although it is really past. In this way there arises, for reflection, a distinction between past and future *in the past.* Now by analogy with this I may project myself in imagination into the future, to the 'end of time' if I please, and in that case I must think what is really the future as if it were already past. This must mean that I think the future as already determinate; and some of its determinations I may be prepared to specify theoretically. I call this theoretical determination of the future 'prediction', if I believe I have sufficient grounds in my knowledge of the past to offer for it, and 'prophecy' if I only have 'a hunch'. In this way there arises the conception of the future as already determinate; and of all time as an order of determination, that is to say, as already past. Time as a determinate sequence of events is necessarily past time; it is indeed the conception of the past, and the distinction of past and future in it is the relative distinction which arises by a theoretical selection of a point in time as the present. This is clearly possible only theoretically; and if it is taken otherwise it implies that the Self exists as subject, but not as agent. Theoretically I can select any point in time I please as the present, and call what came before it the past and what came after it the future. But as agent the present is determined for me. It is the 'here-and-now', my only point of action, for I can act neither in the past nor in the future. And even in reflection, I can only *think* here and now; and my ability to place myself in thought at any point in time I please depends on the fact that all points in time are represented here and now, for my reflection, simultaneously. Now an order of simultaneity is spatial. In so far then as time is a given order within which events can be assigned to determinate positions, the time is past time, and the determination is a theoretical determination. A determinate future is not a real future. The real future is the indeterminate which is determined in action, and in being determined becomes the past. The physicist's time is not real time; it is time represented as past, without a future.

Now let us turn to another implication of action, which we can best formulate in the proposition that *action is choice*. Consider again our solitary agent in empty space. He is aware of space as the possibility of moving in an infinite number of directions from his present position. But if he moves, it must be in one of these directions and in no other. He cannot move in several directions at once. Now since action is irreversible, when he acts, and so moves in one of the possible directions, all the others become, by his action, impossible. His action, then, is a choice of one possibility which negates the possibility of all the others. They become past possibilities, which are no longer actually possible. To do anything is to do *this and not that*. After it is done I may wish I had done something else, but I cannot do it. What I have done remains actual and I cannot undo it. Action is thus the actualizing of a possibility, and as such it is choice. It is important to notice that this means precisely what it says. It does not mean that an action is preceded by a choice;

nor that a mysterious 'act of will' somehow connects a theoretical selection with a physical movement. This is only an attempt to construe the mystery of action from a dualist point of view. There may indeed, in particular cases, be a reflective activity which precedes action, and which consists in deciding, between a number of alternative courses, which is the right course to pursue. But this is only a theoretical, not an actual choosing; as is shown by the fact that the action so 'chosen' may not in fact be performed. The actual choice is the doing of the action; and action is choice whether or not this preliminary reflection takes place. There can, undoubtedly, be no choosing apart from reflection; but this need only be that primary reflection which is in action, as one of its dimensions.

That action is choice discloses another implication of action which it is important to clarify. The distinction between right and wrong is inherent in the nature of action. Knowingly to actualize one of a number of possibles, and in doing so to negate the others, is to characterize the act that is so performed as right and the others as wrong. Again, it is the doing of the action which so distinguishes between right and wrong, not a theoretical judgement which may or may not precede, accompany or follow the doing. Consequently, if we may say that a proposition is that which can be true or false, we may also say that an action is what can be right or wrong. The question which underlies any philosophical inquiry into action is, 'How can I do what is right?' It is not, 'How can we know what it is right to do?' If this second question were to prove unanswerable, it would not follow that the first question was so too. The belief that we can only do what is right by first knowing what it is right to do and then doing this is an assumption. It implies the very principle which Kant was so rightly concerned to deny, that the good can be determined as an object in time. For it presupposes in ourselves two capacities to neither of which we can lay claim—theoretical infallibility and practical omnipotence. If I am to do what is right by first deciding what it is right to do in the circumstances in which I must act, my moral judgement must be infallible. If not, I may be mistaken, and if I then do what I judge mistakenly to be right, not merely have I done wrong, but I could not have done otherwise. But this is not all. Suppose we grant to ourselves this infallibility of moral judgement, what follows? I know absolutely, before I act, what I ought to do. If I then seek to do it, I may fail. Circumstances over which I have no control may intervene, and I discover, in the event, that what I have done is not what I set out to do. Again I have not done what is right; and again I could not have done it. Whatever may be true of our ability to judge what is right—and can we really believe that it is not liable to error?— it is certainly untrue that we have an absolute power to carry out our decisions and achieve our objectives. In some sense, 'ought' implies 'can'. In some sense, therefore, if we can act rightly, it must be without a prior theoretical determination of what it is right to do. The discrimination of right and wrong in action must be prior to and not dependent upon the theoretical discrimination of the truth or falsity of a judgement.

This may seem incomprehensible; and it is indeed one way of exhibiting what Kant called the incomprehensibility of freedom, and of deducing from it, as he did, the primacy of practical reason. We have seen earlier that this incomprehensibility arises from the confrontation of the two antithetical standpoints in the Critical philosophy—the 'I think' and the 'I do'. Since we have decided to stand firmly on the 'I do' and to take up the 'I think' into it as its negative aspect, we have a right to expect that this incomprehensibility is not final. We cannot, however, proceed now to resolve the paradox. For though we are seeking to overcome the purely theoretical standpoint of our philosophical tradition, we are still accepting its egocentricity. The Self as agent is still solitary and self-contained; and this makes it impossible to throw light on this darkness until we come to discuss the interrelation of persons. For the present we must put up with the paradox. What we can do now is to show why the solitary self, even as agent, cannot provide the possibility of action. In actuality, the solitary self can only mean the Self in reflection, self-isolated from the world, withdrawn into itself. This is the Self in self-negation, the negative aspect of selfhood, or the Self as subject. The standpoint of the solitary self, if that Self is considered to be actual or existent, is therefore necessarily the theoretical standpoint.

We have been considering the agent as solitary in empty space and time. We recognized that this was an abstraction, legitimate for methodological purposes. Let us now ask in what this abstraction consists; and in particular why, even as an abstraction, it is inadequate for its purpose, which was to exhibit the characteristics of action in the simplest possible form. It has yielded certain fundamental conclusions: that action is the realization of possibility; that it is therefore choice; and that the distinction between right and wrong is inherent in it. Now we must notice that the abstraction to which we committed ourselves negates all these characteristics; because in the conditions we have supposed no action is possible. The reason is that we have abstracted from the presence of the Other, and therefore from the possibility of resistance in action; and we have already seen that it is the experience of resistance that establishes the distinction of Self and Other. Without an other there can be no self. Without a resistance there can be no action.

We postulated a solitary self in time and space: but we found that time and space are nothing in themselves; and when we took them as mere forms they resolved themselves into the forms of action and of reflection respectively. As such they are the forms of the positive and negative aspects of the existence of the Self. But since the Self is the correlate of the Other, they must equally be forms of the existence of the Other in its positive and negative aspects; as acting upon the Self and being known by the Self. If then there is to be a self there must also be an other in space and time. The Self cannot exist in isolation.

We said that if the Agent moved in any direction, his action chose that direction as the right direction by negating all the other possible directions of movement. We can recognize the inadequacy of our abstract representation if we say that this must mean that whatever the agent does will be right because he does it. No action can then be wrong, and where wrong action is impossible right action is equally impossible. An action is that which can be right or wrong. This really signifies that without an other no action is possible. The scientific analogue of this is the relativity of motion. No movement in space can be determined, and therefore no position in space, except by reference to a fixed point independently determined. Our hypothetical agent in empty space could not discriminate possible directions of movement, because there is no ground for discrimination outside himself. Any one movement would then be identical with any other. There is, however, one way in which we might introduce a ground of discrimination without actually referring to the existence of the Other. Suppose that the Agent is, as agent, already in motion. Then there is one direction of movement which is, by this fact, discriminable. It is the direction which continues, without alteration, the movement already begun. This then would be the right course for the agent to pursue; but since it would also be the only course for which any ground of discrimination existed, it would also be the only possible course. Because of this however we should not call it an action but merely the continuance of an action already initiated.

We see here the origin of Newton's first law of motion and the ground of its abstract certainty. We derive the standpoint of physical science from our experience of action by eliminating from the latter the rational aspect—knowledge, and the organic aspect—reaction to stimulus. What remains is the material world—the displacement of masses in space. If we first suppress the Other from the experience of action, and conceive the agent as isolated in space, and then eliminate knowledge and reaction to stimulus from the conception of the agent, we have Newton's particle moving in space in complete isolation. The first law of motion follows. The particle will continue to move in the same direction without any change. Its movement will continue unaltered. If now we conceive the Other in general, as non-rational and inorganic, we conceive a material world. For the reasons indicated, I propose to call this the conception of the Other as the Continuant, in contrast to the Self as the Agent.

If we conceive the Agent, not as isolated in empty space but as alone in a material world, we provide an element of resistance to support action. The Other, as continuant, offers a resistance to the movement of the Agent, and so makes actual movement by the Agent possible. Is this sufficient to provide the possibility of action? The answer must be negative. The resistance of the continuant is a negative resistance, and the support it provides is a negative support. It provides for the possibility of *movement*, but not of *action*. For though the resistance limits the possibilities for the agent it still provides no ground for discriminating between the possibilities which remain open. Within the limits of his freedom the agent can still do as he pleases, and whatever he does will be right because he does it. He has the means of action, but no ground of action; for the material environment as such does not serve to discriminate between possible objectives.

This merely elaborates the general principle that Self and Other are correlative. If the Other is conceived in purely material terms then the Self must be similarly conceived. If then we make the Self an organism, we cannot leave the Other a mere material world, a mere system of physical energy. We shall have to conceive it as an organic environment, as Nature, itself adapted to provide the means of life for living creatures, and to provide stimuli which will awaken in them the responses through which they adapt themselves to her, and in which their life consists. If then we grant the agent an organic environment, something more than movement becomes possible, and this something more we call behaviour. Nature will provide stimuli to which he can respond. But *action* is still impossible. For at most the knowledge of Nature will reveal a plurality of possible activities, some easier, some more difficult, some pleasurable and some painful. But this still provides no ground of discrimination. At most the agent could 'follow the line of least resistance', and this excludes the determination of an objective. If we say that natural teleology prescribes an objective, the preservation of his life and the avoidance of death, we are brought up short by the fact that the agent knows that this is an impossible objective. Death is unavoidable; consequently any choice of self-preservation as objective of action is inherently irrational. The biblical story of the Fall is quite correct in linking the knowledge of good and evil with the knowledge 'Thou shall surely die'. The solitary agent for whom the Other is an organic environment can only behave as an organism, responding to environmental stimuli. He cannot act: he could at most know the complete futility of all his behaviour through an objective consciousness which accompanied, but was not integrated with it.[1]

We are left with one possible conclusion. The possibility of action depends upon the Other being also agent, and so upon a plurality of agents in one field of action. The resistance to the Self through which the Self can exist as agent must be the resistance of another self. The distinction between right and wrong depends upon a clash of wills. How the relation of persons in action makes action possible cannot, as has been said, be determined at this stage of our argument. That it must be so we are at liberty to affirm, since other possibilities are excluded, and the 'I do'—the fact that there is action—is the primary certainty.

[1] This is one of the permanent themes of Existentialism; and it arises in Existentialism because the organic concept of the Self has not been overcome.

CHAPTER SEVEN

Causality and the Continuant

Any inquiry must begin from *prima facie* distinctions within its field of study, and from the most general distinctions. It must start, that is to say, with a classification of its data. The principle of this classification must have a *prima facie* validity. By this is meant that there must be good reasons for adopting this rather than any other principle as our method of discrimination, so far as our knowledge goes; although, as the inquiry progresses we may have to discard it in favour of another. In a philosophical inquiry the field is unlimited; consequently we must start from a *prima facie* distinction of universal application. The distinction between 'mental' and 'material' is such a *prima facie* principle. We may formulate it thus: 'Everything without exception is either material or mental and nothing can be both.' We might call this a *prima facie* principle of metaphysical classification.

We have seen reason, in reflecting upon the development of modern philosophy, to discard this particular principle of classification. There are *prima facie* grounds for its adoption only from a merely theoretical standpoint. From the new point of view which we have adopted, a new classificatory principle is needed. Now the new point of view, being that of the Agent, is practical; consequently, the distinguishable elements in experience are activities, not objects; while for primary awareness—for knowledge in action—they are changes. Now there is a *prima facie* distinction, of unlimited application, which we use for classifying changes. All changes, we assume, are either 'acts' or 'events'; either they are 'doings' or they are 'happenings'. Further, this distinction between what is done and what happens is exclusive and exhaustive. Any change is either an event or an act, and no change can be both. This then, would seem to be the *prima facie* distinction of which we are in search.

It might seem that to substitute the distinction of 'act' and 'event' for the traditional distinction between 'mind' and 'matter' is merely to exchange one form of dualism for another. Now from a merely theoretical point of view this is indeed the case. As concepts, 'act' and 'event' exclude one another. Indeed, we have already seen that the mind-matter dualism is the theoretical reflection of the dualism between theory and practice. But what is a dualism from the theoretical point of view is not necessarily so from the practical. The experience of the Self as agent, we have discovered, requires, for its representation, a form in which a positive includes and is constituted by its own negative. *Prima facie*, therefore, what happens must be taken as the negative aspect of what is done. The 'I do', as the primary datum, is positive: the 'it happens' must then be the included negative. One of the most familiar examples of this relation of 'doing' and 'happening' is the actual experience of thinking. Thinking is something that I do; yet when I think, my thoughts appear to develop themselves in me in a necessary fashion; and any new discovery I make in thinking appears to happen of itself, in 'a flash of insight or inspiration' which I must wait for, and cannot command at will. I find myself saying 'Suddenly the thought struck me'. Yet I am well aware, that unless I had been thinking, and indeed thinking hard and attentively, the thought would not have struck me. This is not, however, a peculiarity of reflection. In all our actions there is included much that merely happens. If this were not so, nothing could ever be done. When I decide to do anything, the necessary co-ordination of nervous and muscular activities which the intention requires happens automatically, and is included in the doing of what I intend.

Now 'act' and 'event' are practical concepts, and the distinction between them is a practical distinction. From a purely theoretical point of view both are merely apprehended changes; perhaps changes in a visual field. A change is *in itself*, as apprehended, neither 'act' nor 'event'. I mean by this, that it is the mere substitution of one appearance for another. To call it either 'act' or 'event' is to refer beyond it to something else which 'produces' it. No inspection of a change, however minute and careful, will of itself determine whether it was 'done' or merely 'happened'; indeed, inspection cannot even suggest either of these concepts. In practice we sometimes find ourselves unable to decide whether a change is an event or an act. Is the noise of a door closing in the night due to a burglar in the house or just to the wind? The question can be settled only by further evidence. In a word, to call anything either an event or an act is to refer beyond what is observed to an activity—an expenditure of energy—of which it is the product. Apart from such a practical reference it is neither the one nor the other. It is this fact which gives rise to the conception, whether legitimate or not, of pure contingency. A purely contingent occurrence would be an observed change which was neither an act nor an event; something that could not be referred beyond itself to a 'source' or 'origin'; something for which nothing at all was responsible, and which could not therefore be accounted for.

To call any apprehended change an 'act' is to refer it to an agent as its source. To call it an event is to refer it to a non-agent. We express the distinction between acts and events, therefore, if we say: for an event there is a cause; for an act there is a reason. If we believe a change to be an event, and wish to understand it, we must ask, 'What caused it?'; if we think it an act, we have to ask, 'Who did it, and why did he do it?' The explanation of an event is the discovery of the cause which produced it; the explanation of an act is the discovery of the reason for its performance. The cause stands to the event as the reason stands to the act. But since to call an occurrence an event is to refer it to a cause; and to call it an act is to refer it to a reason, we can formulate the general principles involved in two universal assertions. For every event there is a cause; for every act there is a reason. And since the distinction of 'act' and 'event' is a principle of ultimate or metaphysical classification, and institutes a conceptual dualism, we must recognize that the distinction between 'reason' and 'cause' is an absolute distinction; so that no act can have a cause; and no event a reason. At the same time we must remember that 'act' and 'event' are existential concepts. An imagined event is an event which does not occur; an imagined act, even if the agent has decided to do it, is an act which has not, and may never take place. It is an obvious corollary of this that it is nonsensical to ask what is the cause of an act, or the reason for an event. The assertion that every event has a cause does not contradict the assertion that no act has a cause; it implies this.

Though we are concerned here with the distinction of act and event only, we should, for the sake of completeness, interpose a word or two about organic changes, where there is ground for a distinction between the principle of cause and effect, and the principle of stimulus and reaction. The difference lies, as we noted already, in this—that we understand the behaviour of organisms teleologically, in terms of adaptation. We do not, however, assign a reason for the behaviour but only a motive. For even if consciousness enters into its determination, this consciousness is motive and not cognitive. It is important, for this reason, to distinguish two senses in which the notion of teleology may be employed, and which are often confused. In both cases we account for a process of change by reference to an end. In one case, however, the process is determined by a knowledge of the end, while in the other knowledge is not a determinant of the process, and even if present does not enter into our account of the process. In understanding organic behaviour teleologically our point of reference is the end actually or normally occurring as the final stage of the process. We determine the process as a series of successive changes necessary to reach this end. In understanding deliberate human behaviour teleologically, on the other hand, our point of reference is not the end actually reached, but the end proposed to himself or intended by the agent, and we understand the process of action as a successful or unsuccessful attempt to realize this intention, which is the agent's reason for acting as he has acted. As a result of this we judge, if he is successful, that he has done the right thing; if unsuccessful that he has made a mistake, or acted wrongly. These two types of process have, therefore, quite distinct logical forms. If we confuse them it is because of an ambiguity in the term 'end'. As it is essential to avoid this confusion, the term 'teleology' should be restricted to its original and proper use, which lies in the description and comprehension of organic behaviour. Action is not teleological, but intentional. It is described and understood by reference to the purpose of an agent.

If we make this distinction clearly, organic behaviour is brought within the field of what happens, in any *prima facie* distinction we draw between acts and events. If the limitation of teleological categories to the organic field seems to anyone to be merely a verbal device for avoiding awkward questions, we must insist that this is not the case. For though some classes of acts are properly described and understood by reference to an end, this is by no means true of all acts. It is possible only where the end is determinate before action begins and remains unmodified throughout the process of acting. The end of an action, being matter of intention and not matter of fact, is in principle indeterminate. It is not actual, but determinable by the agent in action. The general who determined the movements of his troops in a battle before action was joined, and who maintained his intention throughout the battle whatever the enemy did, would deserve to lose the battle, and almost certainly would. The inability to alter one's plans as a changing situation demands is a form of stupidity: the refusal to do so is the kind of practical stupidity which we call obstinacy or pig-headedness. In principle, therefore, action in general cannot be defined teleologically, even if there is always a teleological element contained in it. It can be defined only as an activity informed by knowledge. Since time is the form of action this knowledge has a necessary reference to the future. The 'I do' is in any actual case an 'I do x'. But to the question, 'What is x?' that is, 'What are you doing?' though some answer must be possible, it is not necessarily a very determinate answer; and in principle can never be completely determinate, but only to a greater or lesser degree. The agent can always change his mind. I may answer the question, 'What are you doing?' by saying, 'I'm walking eastwards.' If then the questioner says, 'Yes, but where are you going?' I may reply, 'I don't know yet; I haven't made up my mind.' The reference to the future must be sufficient to determine a direction of advance; it need not determine an end. And since even the ends which we do determine in action are only relative, since they are also starting-points of further action, we always know to some extent, and never know with full finality, what we are doing.

We may now return to the conception of causality, and consider its relation to action. Since the direction of action, *quâ* action, is determined by the knowledge which is one of its dimensions, it is understood by reference to this knowledge; that is to say, by discovering the reason why the agent did it. If we know this reason fully, then we understand the action fully. (The negative which must qualify this we shall consider presently.) This is the primary understanding we possess, from which all other forms of the understanding of activity must be derived by limitation. An event, therefore, is a change which cannot be referred to an agent as its source. It is not directed by knowledge; consequently no reason can be given for it. The idea of an event is the idea of an action, from which the element of knowledge has been excluded. The personal experience which is the necessary model for this, is twofold. In the first place, there are organic activities of our own, which though teleological, are yet 'unconscious' or automatic. These may or may not be accompanied by knowledge; but if they are, the knowledge does not determine them, and is not integrated with our own movements. Secondly, there is our experience of 'accidents'. Accidents, though they form part of the observable process of our movements in action are not integrated with it, and cannot be referred to any intention of ours. If, for instance, I accidentally drop and break a glass which I am carrying, the breakage is produced by me, yet is not an act of mine. The question, 'Why did you break that glass?' has no answer, and is inadmissible. I should reply, 'I didn't; it was a pure accident.' Here is an occurrence in which I am implicated, yet which cannot be referred to my intention as its source. We may notice here, though it is not strictly relevant, that this distinction between act and accident can never be determined by any inference from observed fact. The inference from fact to intention is always formally invalid. The evidence is always in principle circumstantial. Yet the conclusion may be certain, for all that. The extra-logical element in any proof of intention is an analogy from our own experience as agents. Further, even when we are convinced that there was no intention present, we may still suspect an unconscious motive. If so, the accident is to be understood teleologically, as a phenomenon of motive consciousness, as a case of organic causality. We must note however that such determination by unconscious motives is unintentional. There can be no such thing as an unconscious *intention*. The term 'intention', at least in a context like the present, always implies knowledge determining action.

Now when no reason can be assigned for an observed change, and it is therefore not an act, we call it an 'event' and refer it to a 'cause'. What then do we mean by a 'cause'? We mean the source of an occurrence which stands to an event as an agent stands to his act, but which is not an agent. Since in any attempt to understand events the conception of cause must be thought positively, we must say that a cause is a source of occurrences which is a non-agent; an existent which is other than an agent.

The conception of 'cause' is inherently self-contradictory. It is the conception of an agent that is not an agent, the negation of agency. The negative, we know, cannot exist independently, but only as the negative aspect of a positive in the form of the personal. Within action, which is a personal concept, there not merely can, but must be a negation of action; but this negation is in the last analysis a self-negation. If the negative aspect is thought as existing independently of the positive, the result is a contradiction. We think the non-existent as existing. The difficulties of any theory of causation arise from this. The conception of cause both includes and excludes the idea of the 'production' of an effect. In consequence, whatever we assign as the cause of an event is something which is not in itself capable of producing an effect, but only, as it were, of transmitting it. It is a means through which something else produces the occurrence. In other words, the 'cause' turns out to be merely another event which must be itself referred to another cause. An infinite regress of causes faces us in every case. This is what is meant when people say that a causal explanation only tells us *how* things happen, and not *why* they happen; or better still that it describes the course of events without explaining it.

So long as the use of the notion of cause falls within action and so has a practical reference, it is meaningful and indispensable. For in such cases it refers to a negative activity which falls within the positive activity of an actual agent. The case of ill-health or disease, whether 'mental' or 'organic', is presumably the primary instance; for then the organic functioning of the body or its motive consciousness is clearly a negative aspect of action. But the same is true of tools, instruments or machines which we construct for our use, and which are means for the transmission of our own energy, and so in a sense extensions of our own bodies. A breakdown in these, as in our own organic functioning, leads us to ask for its cause. The question is now a practical one, and the term 'cause' refers to that which we must alter by our action in order to restore our capacity to act through the instrument.[1]

When however we are concerned with purely theoretical

[1] This aspect of the matter has been admirably dealt with in an important article by the late Professor R. G. Collingwood in the *Procceedings of the Aristotelian Society* for 1937–8 (N.S., Vol. XXXVIII), under the title 'On the So-called Idea of Causation'.

construction, the contradiction is a mere source of embarrassment, and scientific theory therefore seeks to replace it by a less objectionable notion, from which the idea of 'production' is at least more remote. This is the idea of natural law. Instead of inquiring for the cause of an event, we ask for a law in accordance with which it happens. This idea of a law of Nature is, of course, anthropomorphic, in the bad sense of the term. A law is a general prescription which an agent issues for the actions of another agent; and since the other *is* an agent he can choose to disregard it. In all strictness no agent can *compel* another agent to do anything; he can at most provide what he hopes will prove a sufficient motive to determine the other agent's choice of the desired course of action. A law of Nature is said to be not prescriptive but merely descriptive. Strictly speaking it is not a law at all; but in calling it a law we are thinking of it as a prescription which in the nature of the case can never be disregarded. The idea of descriptive law is perhaps too well established to provoke serious misunderstanding in science. But its emotional effect is the more objectionable that it is unconscious; serving to maintain an attitude of misplaced reverence for Nature as the Lawgiver, which echoes an ancient worship; and to invest the professional scientist with magical powers for the salvation of the world. The scientists, of course, make no such superstitious claims; yet they would be hardly human if they did not enjoy and even profit by the adulation of the vulgar. It is desirable that this atavism should be exorcised; for it would be a pity, and might even prove disastrous, if in an age in which the influence of the higher religions is declining, the primitive faiths which they overcame should again revive.

The notion of natural law rests upon the concept of the Other as continuant, that is to say, as non-agent in process. We must therefore consider this notion of the 'continuant' more closely. To continue is to remain unchanged throughout a period of time. Continuance then is the character of having a being in time that does not alter; and the continuant is that which persists without change. The simplest form of continuance is the occupation of a position for a time without change. But as this is a negative and unreal or purely abstract notion we may disregard it in favour of movement in a straight line. This is what is defined in Newton's first law of motion. The movement of a particle in empty space is an instance of simple continuance. But all continuance is not in this fashion simple. The movement of a particle with a constant acceleration—as defined, for instance, by Newton's law of gravitation—is equally an instance of continuance. Here there is change of velocity, but the rate of change of velocity remains unchanged. Again, the oscillation of a pendulum with a frictionless pivot, is equally a continuance, because the to and fro motion continues without alteration; and if we take into account the friction of the pivot, there is still a continuance, since the decrease of the amplitude of the oscillation is constant. This enables us to define continuance in a way that is applicable to all cases, however complex. Wherever there is something, whatever it may be, which is a recurrence of the same, we are in the presence of a continuant.

Now it is clear that there is an intimate relation between the idea of continuance, and the idea of natural law. If we ask what it is that a law of Nature describes the answer must be a recurrent pattern of change. Consider again the oscillating pendulum, and suppose a complete absence of frictional interference with its movement. The pendulum then swings from A to B, and back again to A along the arc of a circle whose radius is the distance from its pivot. This movement has a positive and a negative phase, and these phases are equal and opposite. The whole movement, from A back to A, recurs without change *ad infinitum*, in the absence of all interference. If we limit our attention to one complete swing we can determine this by measurement. We need only measure the length of the radius, the angle subtended by the arc at the pivot, and the time that elapses during the complete swing. We can combine these measurements in a suitable mathematical formula. If we then add the assertion that this formula applies without modification to any complete swing of the pendulum we have determined the particular law which governs the oscillation of that pendulum. We see from this that we can determine the whole movement of the pendulum *ad infinitum* by determining any part of it which exhibits a completed pattern of change—in this case the rhythm of the oscillation; and we can do this because this rhythmic pattern recurs *ad infinitum* without change. The result is that from this law, which is our mathematical formulation of the pattern, we can predict the position of the pendulum at any future time we please.

We can go farther than this, however. We need not suppose the impossible condition of a complete absence of friction. We may measure the friction actually present in a particular pendulum. Provided we assume that this friction is constant we can incorporate the coefficient of friction in our formula. If however this, too, is presupposing ideal conditions, since the wear and tear on the pivot must modify the friction, we may measure the rate of change of friction, and assuming that *this* is constant, we may complicate our formula still further by including this constant also. The farther we proceed in this direction, the closer our formula approximates to the conditions actually found in Nature, and the more exact do our predictions become. The determination of laws of Nature, then, depends upon the discovery of natural constants; that is to say, upon natural continuance.

The laws of which we have been speaking are particular laws; but what is usually meant by a law of Nature is general. These general laws of Nature are derived from the particular laws by generalization. From the formula for a particular frictionless pendulum we can derive a formula for all frictionless pendulums. For in all cases, though some elements vary, others remain constant. If this were not so they could not be instances of the oscillation of a pendulum. The formulae of the different instances then will exhibit constant elements and variable elements. We can therefore devise a general formula in which the constant elements provide the determinate structure and the variables are represented by special symbols. This is our general law, which can be applied, in any particular case, by determining the value of the variables for that case. In other words the law of a particular instance can be derived from the general law, by determining what is variable in it. The general law holds for all instances of a class. If we ask, then, what makes them all instances of a class, the answer will be that the general law applies to them all. If this seems to beg the question—and in a sense it does—we must refer to what has already been said about classification. Clearly before we can determine a general law, we must have a principle of classification which is independent of it. But this principle need only be *prima facie*: it may require modification as our knowledge progresses. Observed resemblances may provide a rough starting-point: but in view of what has already been said about the secondary character of the 'observational' point of view, it would be at least more fundamental to say that we begin by classifying together all instances in relation to which we find in practice that we can act successfully in the same fashion. The original constants are to be found in our own modes of action, for which, of course, perceptual resemblances are an original, if somewhat untrustworthy guide.

A 'law of Nature', then, is a pattern of continuance, and the discovery of such 'laws' is the discovery of such patterns in our experience of the Other. To say of any group of phenomena that it obeys a law is to assert that it contains a pattern of change which recurs without change. To say that Nature in general obeys laws, or that all phenomena occur in accordance with laws, is to assert that Nature is the Continuant, or the non-agent in temporal existence.

There are certain observations to be made concerning the process whereby our first practical discrimination of the world is developed through reflection into a scientific understanding of Nature and so confers upon our practical activity a wider range and an increasing exactitude. We must notice that however far we carry it, the process depends upon the isolation of recurrent patterns. This has two results which render our conclusions uncertain and liable to endless revision. The first of these is that an element of idealization is always present. In speaking of the law which is obeyed by a frictionless pendulum, we were isolating the phenomena which exhibit the recurrent pattern from all phenomena of friction. The result is that we consider an ideal case, which can never be actual. But if we then include the element of friction we are still isolating the phenomena included from other phenomena with which the swinging pendulum is in fact inseparably connected; and the case is still idealized. For practical purposes we can isolate the phenomena in accordance with a principle of relevance, so that the elements excluded are negligible *for our purposes*. But theoretically the isolation of elements within the whole must produce an ideal case which is never fully actual, and the 'laws' which we thus establish apply in principle only subject to a qualification. Actual instances vary from the ideal case within limits. This is at least part of what is meant when it is said that all scientific laws are statistical. Even such a simple determination as that water is H_2O, is the setting up of an ideal norm, and water which precisely conforms to this rule can only be produced in the laboratory, if even there.

The second result concerns the predictions which we base upon these 'laws'. They must be made with the qualification, expressed or understood, 'provided nothing interferes'. The prediction is made on the basis of an ideal isolation from the actual complexity of conditions to which it refers and in which it must be realized. There is therefore always a possibility that some of the factors left out of our calculation may interfere with the realization of our prediction. In the case of the pendulum, we may calculate the time at which it will come to rest, but only with the proviso that nothing interferes with its freedom to swing; that is to say, provided the conditions obtaining when we took our measurements remain constant. This we can never guarantee; although in some cases we may be able to calculate with fair accuracy the probability of a change in the conditions.

This possibility of interference becomes of special importance if we take account of the presence of agents and their intentions. I can calculate when my pendulum will come to rest; but also I can stop it myself at any moment; or I can arrange a mechanism which will keep it swinging indefinitely. The range and accuracy of astronomical predictions, and the high degree of certainty they possess depends largely upon the fact that we know of no agents who have the power, even had they the will, to interfere. It is important, therefore, to notice this special case of the possibility of personal interference. All our physical predictions depend on an abstraction from the presence of agents, with their capacity to determine the future. We must postulate a world in which there is no action; and such a world is itself an ideal isolate, a world in which there are no persons. But this can never be the actual world in which we operate. For the process of determining the patterns of recurrence is itself a personal activity which requires experiment; and an experiment is itself a deliberate personal interference with the processes which are observed. What we call the physical world is, therefore, in all strictness, an imaginary world. Even in conception, it is the world which we know, of which we are part and in which we act imagined as existing without ourselves or any other agents whatsoever in it; a world in which there is no action. Indeed, if we are referring to the world as conceived by the physicist, it is a world also in which there are no organisms and therefore no responses to stimulus; a world, therefore, in which there are no stimuli to which an organism might respond.

Now consider the experimental situation without abstraction. To determine the law which governs the movement of the pendulum, I erect a pendulum, and I set it swinging. Then I begin to take the measurements I need. But during the experiment I do not interfere with its motion. My practical concern is to keep the conditions constant throughout—to prevent interference. When I have made all the measurements I require, I stop the pendulum, and sit down to study the measurements I have noted. The whole experiment is an action of mine: I *do* the experiment. But the pattern of movement I observe and the law that I elicit, refer only to what happens *within* my action. I leave out of account my starting the pendulum when I begin and my stopping it when I have finished. The law of the particular instance refers to what happens between these points; to that aspect of my doing the experiment which I do not *do*; that is to say, the negative aspect of my action. If now we call this a causal process, we realize in another way that causality is the negative aspect of agency, and falls within action.

The 'I do', we see again, is the necessary starting-point. The 'it happens' falls within it in actuality, and in conception is abstracted from it. I can always ask, 'What happens when I do something?' when I drive a car from Glasgow to Edinburgh, for example. The question refers to all the elements in my action which do themselves, as it were; which are not determined by a deliberate and specific intention of my own. Consequently a complete account of my journey is possible, which nowhere refers to any intention of mine. If we please, we need not even refer to my bodily movements; but confine the record to the movements of the mechanism of the car. Or, if we please, we can include the movements of my hands on the steering wheel and gear lever, and of my feet on the pedals. Or again, we may include reference to my automatic reflexes and responses to stimuli. All these accounts are made possible by a deliberate choice to refrain from asking certain questions, which in fact are quite legitimate, and which are indeed necessary to a complete understanding. We keep within the field of happening by excluding questions which involve a reference to agency. The moment we ask, 'Why were you going to Edinburgh anyway?' the tracing of causal processes or continuant patterns must stop, because the answer must refer to an intention. 'Because I live in Edinburgh,' might be a sufficient answer.

We have taken our examples of continuance from the physical field, for simplicity's sake. But this does not imply that the organic and personal fields do not equally exhibit continuance. In the organic field indeed it is most immediately impressive. The repetition of the life cycle in successive generations, 'each according to his kind', has always attracted human attention and interest. Here we clearly find a pattern of change which *prima facie* repeats itself without change. The theory of an evolution of species requires no modification in principle. If it is spontaneous, then the repetition with variation is itself the pattern which repeats, and the principle of the successive variations is itself determinable. But it seems more likely that the larger variations, and perhaps all variations from type, have their ground in some interference, or in some change in environmental conditions. The belief that organic development is also determined in accordance with natural law; or—which is in the end the same thing—that for a particular organism the pattern of response to stimulus is determinate, is not merely based upon observation. It is a necessity for thought. For the only spontaneous initiation of change which we can conceive is the act of an agent; and whatever is non-agent, that is to say, non-personal, must be conceived as a continuant. Without a ground of change, the movement which has been begun must continue without change.

In the personal field this organic continuance appears as habitual activity. Our habits are those elements in our practical activity which are recurrent responses to recurrent stimuli. They differ from instinctive reactions only in the fact that they have to be learned in the first instance, and consequently can, in principle, be unlearned. Normally our habits are continuously qualified by the intentional action within which they fall and which they make possible. All actions depend upon a system of habitual responses to stimuli; and the formation of habits is the necessary basis of every action. If we cross a busy street, we concentrate our attention upon our objective and upon traffic to be avoided, and determine the direction, the changes of direction and the timing of our movements. The rest—and it is the greater part—of our activity is automatically adapted to these conscious determinations. Here habit is clearly the negative aspect of our action, without which the action could not take place. It is integrated with and subservient to the positive aspect of deliberate purpose in terms of which the action must be defined. This can be clearly seen by contrast with abnormal cases in which a habit becomes compulsive, and escapes from deliberate control. Only then do we find an activity which is *purely* habitual, and for which the agent is not immediately responsible.

Such an autonomous habit is a behaviour pattern which recurs without change. It follows that if we can determine the pattern, we can formulate a law which will enable us to predict the future behaviour of the agent in respect of every recurrence of the particular stimulus to which the habit is a response. Now suppose that this particular autonomous habit is common to a group of persons, or to all persons. Then the law of the habit could be generalized, and the behaviour of all agents in the group could in this respect be predicted. Suppose then that we proceed as psychologists, in precisely the same way as the physicist does, by abstracting from action and considering only that aspect of personal behaviour which is constituted by habit. We can then study the activities of persons *as if they were purely continuant*. We can make experiments with normal persons who will agree to behave in accordance with our instructions, and not for their own ends and on their own initiative. In this way we can isolate, under laboratory conditions, those aspects of human behaviour which would normally be habitual responses within deliberate action. Alternatively, we may study abnormal individuals, suffering from neurotic or psychotic diseases, and so observe actual cases of behaviour which is isolated from normal control by the agent. On the basis of such systematic observation we may seek to determine psychological laws of human behaviour in a thoroughly scientific fashion, and verify them in the usual way. The knowledge that we obtain can be used, just as in the case of physics or biology, for the deliberate control of human behaviour.

We must notice particularly that in these respects there is no difference in principle between psychology and physics, and that the validity of the laws determined in both cases is, in principle, the same. Indeed it is physics which is modelled on psychology in the last analysis and not psychology on physics. For it is our experience of habit in ourselves that provides the notion of a recurrent pattern of change from which the conception of a continuant world obeying laws of Nature is derived, and apart from which it would be inconceivable. The physicist, like the psychologist, abstracts from action—his own action in observing and in making experiments—and so constitutes an ideal world which is purely continuant. That in the one case the continuance is 'external' to the agent and in the other 'internal' makes no essential difference. In both cases the observed continuance falls within action, and is conditioned by action. In both cases verification is through practical control based upon knowledge. Now our control of the continuant in action is in fact easier if it is external to ourselves than if it is internal. It is notoriously difficult to alter our own habits by a deliberate effort. There is no such difficulty in controlling the movements of a material object provided that our knowledge and our available resources are adequate. There is, of course, an empirical difference between the two cases. The patterns of behaviour are much more complex for the psychologist; the difficulty of experiment is greater; the number of instances available is far less, so that the reliability of generalization, even through the use of statistical methods, is greatly diminished. Above all, the probability of interference is very much higher. But these are matters of degree, not of kind.

We shall conclude by noting three important corollaries of this study of the Continuant. Firstly, the substitution of the idea of law for the idea of cause in science does not solve the causal dilemma. It excludes it from consideration by avoiding the question which requires a causal answer. If I observe a process of change I can seek to discover a recurrent pattern in it and so to determine a law of continuance. In doing this, however, I refrain from asking another question, 'What set the process going in the first instance?' This is, of course, the question, 'What is the cause of the process?' and it is not a senseless question, unless we are prepared to deny that the process ever had a beginning. In many cases we can give a definite answer. In the cases in which the process is experimental, the answer is that it didn't need a cause, since somebody performed the experiment. The generality of natural laws consists in the fact that they apply to all particular instances of a kind; and the number of all particular instances is finite. The replacement of the notion of 'cause' by that of 'law' is not properly a *substitution*. It defines a different mode of abstraction or isolation within which the question of a cause does not arise. The incoherence of the conception of 'cause', as an agent which is not an agent, remains unaffected.

The second corollary is this. Since the 'worlds' which are isolated by physics or biology or psychology are imaginary or ideal worlds, we have no ground for asserting that the 'laws' that science formulates apply without qualification to the actual world in which we live. But since these ideal worlds are derived by systematic and well-grounded abstraction, they do fall within the actual world as aspects of it. Since the general abstraction is from action, so that these ideal worlds are systems of continuance, we are justified in saying that the laws of Nature hold of the actual world *in so far as* it is a continuant.

The final corollary is that the Continuant has no future. Time, we have seen, is the form of action. Action distinguishes past from future as the determinate and the undetermined respectively. The determinate is the past, and the continuant is already completely determined. Its temporal determination is that of the spatialized time of which we have spoken, which is the relative time order within the past, and which we can project into the real future in present imagination. The future which we predict for it is really *our* future as agents. Having known it in the past, we shall remember it when we see it again; and what we shall see is what we have already seen. If this is never completely so, it is because the continuant is itself an ideal object. In actual experience it is the negative aspect of action, and thus it gains a relation to real time which in its own right it does not possess.

CHAPTER EIGHT

Reflective Activity

We must now turn to consider the derivation of our theoretical activities, or modes of reflection, from our primary activities which are positive and practical. We have to justify an earlier assertion, that if we start from the 'I think' there is no possibility of arriving at action; whereas it is possible to derive the theoretical from the practical if we affirm the primacy of action. The first step we have already taken, when we recognized that the 'I do' contains the 'I think', of necessity, as its negative aspect. Without knowledge there may be activity, but not action. The 'I do' includes the 'I know that I do'. We must now consider the abstract formula in its concrete setting, as the form of our experience of the world.

The 'I do' is essentially incomplete. In actual experience it must have the form 'I am doing this'. The 'this' again is a specification, which implies discrimination. It means, 'I am doing this and not that.' It answers the question, '*What* am I doing?' Consequently its negative aspect, 'I know that I do', is, in actuality, 'I know that I am doing this and not that'. I must know what I am doing to know that I am acting at all. But, as we have seen, this knowledge of what I am doing is itself incomplete. It admits of greater or less discrimination. I may set out for a walk without knowing where I am going; but not without going in one direction and not in another. I must always know up to a point what I am doing, and never completely. For I am agent in my movement and not merely the cause of it. A cause may initiate a process; thereafter the process continues without control by its cause. But an agent is in his movement, and consequently can always alter or modify it at will within the limits of his resources. If I could know completely what I was doing I should have ceased to be an agent and become a continuant. I should have surrendered my power to modify my intention as I proceed.

This is merely one aspect of the fact that action is choice. The movement of an agent does not happen, it is made; and so long as it is in the making it can be modified. It remains indeterminate throughout until it is complete. On the other hand, an actual choice is possible only if there exists a ground of discrimination independent of the agent. The knowledge in action which makes action possible must therefore be a knowledge of what is practically possible, and of a ground of discrimination between alternative possibilities. In general, then, it must be a knowledge of the Other.

Now the knowledge of the Other is given primarily, we have seen, in action, through tactual perception—as that which resists our intention, and so both limits and supports it. I cannot walk a step without support from the resistance of the ground beneath my feet. If this resistance disappears, I lose the power to move, and must merely fall. For a fall is a movement that happens to me, not a movement that I make. This support for my movement also limits the possible directions of movement. I can move only along the surface of the earth; not upwards or downwards. The knowledge of practical possibility is therefore primarily a knowledge of the variations of resistance to my movement in different directions. The development of this primary knowledge in action is highly complicated, involving as it does the interrelation of tactual perception with the discriminations of bodily feeling, and of our sensory apparatus in general. But this does not concern a philosophical study and must be left to psychology. The discrimination between possibilities, and so choice in action, has its source undoubtedly in our organic needs, which provide the primary intentions of our actions, and so the constant element in the form of all possible intentions.

Instead, then, of pursuing these complications, we may consider the formal difference between human action, even at this primary level, and animal behaviour. This difference lies in the direction of activity by knowledge, and not by mere awareness. What, then, we may ask, is the justification for using the term 'knowledge' in such a context; especially when the traditional usage of modern philosophy would restrict this term to a more exalted use. It would be more normal to speak here of 'immediate awareness' or 'immediate consciousness' or even of 'animal faith', or to use some form of words which would not draw such an extreme contrast between the highest reach of organic consciousness and the lowest level of personal awareness. The justification is that it is precisely to draw such a contrast that the term is used; to mark a distinction of categories which must not be blurred. We have to distinguish absolutely between acting from knowledge, and reacting to a stimulus.

In an earlier chapter we reached the conclusion that conscious reaction to stimulus is motive, and not cognitive, however elaborate the discrimination of consciousness in any reaction to stimulus may be. In any reaction, the initiative of behaviour lies with the stimulus. The reaction involves no choice on the part of the organism. What reaction follows depends, of course, upon the internal structure of the organism, including the structure of its consciousness if consciousness is involved; and since the organism is itself a process of continuous change, it depends also upon the state of the organism at the time the stimulus is applied. Let us call this 'the nature of the organism at the moment'. Then we may say that the reaction is produced by the stimulus in terms of the nature of the organism at the moment. In the case of action, however, the initiative lies with the agent, who determines his activity in terms of the nature of the Other. Suppose that for the moment we take the Other as object, then we must say that awareness in action is an objective awareness; that is, it is the awareness of an object other than the self; and objective awareness is knowledge. It is thus the nature of an agent to act not in terms of his own nature but in terms of the nature of the object, that is, of the Other. However simple and immediate an action may be, so long as it *is* an action, and not merely a reaction to stimulus, then it is informed and directed by an awareness of the Other-than-self *as other*; and the ground of choice, that is, the determination of the action, lies therefore in the agent's knowledge of the Other. This knowledge may be extremely limited; it may be very far from any adequate determination; and however it may be extended in experience, or through reflection, it can never be complete. But so far as it goes it is knowledge and nothing less; and within its limits, however narrow, it is both objective and certain. At the lower limit, the pressure I bring to bear upon an obstacle is an absolute measure of the resistance this other existent offers to my will. It is this experience that enables us to formulate with certainty the principle that 'action and reaction are equal and opposite'. And at a much higher level, if I am asked whether I know the present Prime Minister of Canada, my answer, unless I tell a lie, is necessarily true. I cannot be mistaken. So long as we do not generalize, or anticipate, or in any way go beyond its immediacy, our knowledge of the Other in action has a certainty that no reflective knowledge can ever attain. Indeed, if we limit the term knowledge, as some philosophers would do, to that 'logical certainty' which is the result of theoretical demonstration, we should have to confess that there is not and cannot be knowledge, and so relapse into a complete scepticism. The reference to pure mathematics, which might appear to refute this, is beside the point. For in so far as it is certain it is not knowledge; and in so far as it is knowledge it is not certain. That one plus one equals two is neither true nor false, since it is purely formal and in its purity is strictly meaningless. For it refers to nothing objective. It enunciates a rule for counting; and though a rule may be certain, in the sense that it is the only possible rule for an operation, it cannot be true or false. If however I refer it to the Other, as the form of a judgement about the world, it is no longer certain. If I add one drop of water to another I do not have two drops but only one bigger drop. That the world is constructed on a mathematical plan may conceivably be true, but it is by no means certain, and there is plenty of evidence that appears, at least, to point in the opposite direction.

Since time is the form of action, knowledge in action, which is our primary knowledge, participates in the temporal form. No question arises, therefore, about the way in which we are aware of time itself, as it does for any philosophy which takes the 'Cogito' as primary. If I know that I am doing something then I know *ipso facto* the distinction between past and future which is the form of doing. To be aware of what I am doing while doing it, is to be aware at once both of what I have already done and of what I have yet to do. Such knowledge is therefore, as awareness of the past, memory; and as awareness of the future, anticipation. This reference to the future however is not to matter of fact, but to matter of intention. It implies no affirmation that something will happen; but rather a knowledge of present intention, and an expectation of obstacles which will provide a ground for the continuous modification of intention either in detail or as a whole. No doubt the present intention is determined by an expectation that the present conditions of action will continue; but this is not affirmed. On the contrary, our practical attitude to the future involves an expectancy of continuous change in these conditions necessitating a continuous adaptation of intention. The continuity of the activity of knowing is precisely this concentration of attention upon the unexpected, which leaves to the 'unconscious'—that is, to the automatic reaction to stimulus of the organic awareness which is contained within it—whatever is found to continue without change in the conditions of action. As memory, on the other hand, it is concerned with matter of fact, since what has been done is determinate. The Agent, in determining the future creates a past. As Subject in action he is aware of what he is doing; and this continuous awareness is gathered up from moment to moment as a knowledge of what has now been done and which therefore is eternally determinate and unalterable. The form of this knowledge, memory, involves, of course, the distinction of Self and Other. It is the history of the interrelation of Self and Other up to the present. For the past which the agent creates in action is his own past, in relation to the Other; and the primary awareness of this in memory includes both an awareness of his self-determination and of the Other as his action has determined it.

But now if we abstract from action, and so isolate this knowledge from the action which sustains it, the Self appears as pure subject, knowing an object-world. The Subject stands over against the Object, not in dynamic relation to it; because being the past, no action upon it is possible. And since to abstract from action is to abolish the future, the Subject has no future, quâ subject. This is what is signified when a philosopher asserts that the Subject is not in time, or refers to an 'eternal present'. The empirical analogue of this in psychology is the 'specious present', whose limits are defined at any moment by the memory span of a momentary consciousness. From the standpoint of the agent we must state this differently. The Agent constitutes himself subject by negating his own agency. He forms a theoretical intention. He is then in reflection, turned back upon his own past. This past then is presented in memory as the object of knowledge. It appears as a four-dimensional system, in which time is the fourth dimension. This use of the term 'dimension' is justified, because the time factor in the continuum is the order of past time—the temporal relations of past events all of which are present in memory *at the same time*. It is in this sense that, as we have already noticed, past time is spatialized, as an order of events which coexist for thought in memory. The Subject may select any point he pleases in this time-order as the present, and call what occurred before it past and what occurred after it future, since in abstraction from action there is nothing to determine a real present. He can therefore locate this present in the real future if he pleases; but if he does this he must treat the object-world as merely continuant; and this is always possible. For being the past it is completely determined, and the patterns of its temporal form can be continued in thought indefinitely.

The object of knowledge then is the past conceived as continuant, that is, as completely determinate and not to be modified further by action. This is the 'four-dimensional continuum' of the physicists; or if this use of the term 'dimension' is objected to it is a continuum determined formally by four variables. The activities of reflection, since they are not actions, but 'doings' of the Subject, make no difference to the Object. They merely determine for the Subject in idea what is already determinate in fact. What is given for any particular agent in reflection is only the content of his own memory, which is necessarily fragmentary, and therefore, an indeterminate and very inadequate characterization of the past; or if you will, of what exists. The rational activities of reflection are efforts to extend, and in extending, to correct where necessary the fragmentary content of immediate memory. How this is possible we shall not consider in detail. Kant's account seems to me still to be the best available. We need only remark that from the standpoint of the 'I do' the spatio-temporal framework and the logical determinateness of the structure are no longer postulates of the possibility of experience, but themselves immediate derivatives from our empirical, that is, our practical experience.

We must, however, consider at this point the function of attention in determining the structure of our experience. The 'I do' is experienced as a felt tension in the Self; or rather, since it is an active, not a passive tension, it might be more strictly described as a 'tensing' of the Self. But since the 'I do' is incomplete; and since the Self is the correlate of the Other, this 'tension' is directed towards the Other. This direction, again, has a positive and a negative distinction within it, corresponding to the positive or practical and the negative or reflective aspects of personal experience. In its practical aspect we call it 'intention'; in its reflective aspect 'attention'. We *intend* a modification of the Other, to be determined by our agency. We *attend to* a mode of the other which is already determinate in order that it may reveal to us the structure of its determination. Thus 'intention' and 'attention' refer respectively to the forward-looking and the backward-looking aspects of knowledge in action, to anticipation and memory. In reflective activity there can be no intention, since negative activity determines nothing in reality. The correlative of the reflective self is a continuant world, and its determinateness governs all activities of reflection. We cannot intend the conclusion of a train of thought. We can only attend to what is given, to the data or the premisses. Without this attention nothing happens. With it something follows from the data which is determined by the data, not by any intention of ours. The withdrawal from action is a withdrawal from intending; and so the whole activity of reflection is an activity of attending to what is already there, to what has already been done. Thinking is then something that I do, since without my attention nothing will follow; but it is a negative doing, because what follows when I attend is something that I do not determine. The idealist is right in saying that the idea develops itself in my mind: but this is conditional upon the attention which makes the thinking mine. Apart from this we have mere dreaming, in which the idea develops itself in my mind without any tension in me. Intention, on the other hand contains attention within itself as its negative aspect.

Attention is selective. This is simply the reflective aspect of the fact that action is choice. It can be varied deliberately either in intensity or in concentration. By its intensity I mean the amount of tension in the Self which is involved; by concentration I mean a limiting of the complexity of what is attended to. I may first attend to something as a whole, and then attend to its parts or to aspects of it successively. Again, since attending is what I *do* in reflective activity, I can intend a determinate process of attention. This reflective intention is a negative intention: it cannot determine an end to be achieved, but only a method to be followed in attending. I can formulate a series of questions to be answered through a process of reflection, and decide the order in which they shall be asked. What I cannot do is to determine in advance the answers that I shall get. These have to be discovered. For this reason the success of reflective activity depends largely upon a methodology—upon a systematic ordering of attention.

In its primary character, as attention in action, the selection of what shall be attended to is governed by the intention of the action.[1] In action, we select in attention what is relevant to our intention, or rather what we consider to be relevant. What is not so attended to, so far as it enters into or affects the action, is left to the automatism of habit, that is to say, to the included organic process of response to stimulus. It is the continuant aspect of the situation, that which persists without change, that is excluded from attention. What is attended to is, in the main, the unexpected; for what is expected is already provided for; it is the unexpected—which, of course, is not necessarily the surprising, but simply that which is indeterminable in advance —which is relevant to the modification of intention.

This selectiveness of attention underlies and accounts for those characteristics of reflective activity which are traditionally referred to as 'abstraction' and 'generalization'. Reflective abstraction is a negative 'taking away'; a taking away which in fact takes nothing away. This is possible through a concentration of attention which isolates a discriminable element in a given complex and excludes the rest from consideration. We confine our attention to a part or aspect of a whole. What is so 'abstracted' may of course itself be a complex which in actuality falls within a wider complex. The 'material world', for example, is an abstraction from the actual world in which we act. It is produced by excluding action and confining attention to the continuant aspect of the world. Two important corollaries follow from this. Firstly, what is known in reflection is always

[1] The intention, we must remind ourselves, is not the same thing as the end. It is in the action, and is not fully determinate. The analysis of actions into means and end is reflective, and presupposes that the action is both complete and successful. Our actions are not necessarily planned in advance.

abstract, since it is conditioned by the selectivity of attention; and moreover, reflection is itself constituted by a withdrawal from action. Secondly, the abstract, as such, is non-existent, that is to say, it is *idea*. This is only another way to state Kant's dictum that 'existence is not a predicate'. To exist means to be in dynamic interrelation with other existents. What exists is concrete, not abstract; and existence is a practical experience. That which is isolated from its dynamic relations with the whole, is isolated from existence. Thus reflection is indifferent to the existence of its object. The 'data', or 'facts' upon which reflective activities are directed are abstract. They are primary isolates from practical experience, retained in memory. They are then subject to secondary selection by limitation of attention, since we cannot attend to all the facts we are aware of at once, and must select in accordance with some principle of relevance. So we can produce any possible combination of facts or data in whatever order of attention we please. This is what is sometimes referred to as 'mental construction'; it is a negative construction which consists merely in attending exclusively to a selected group of data; so including their relations to one another, and excluding their relations to anything else from the focus of consciousness. We can combine premises in this way and draw conclusions. But these reflective constructions and the conclusions which follow from them are alike abstract, and carry no guarantee of existence with them. The constructs produced by selective attention, and the conclusions of reflective processes of thought equally require verification by reference to practical experience.

Generalization, again, is itself an aspect of abstraction. Already, in organic reaction to stimulus we find a practical generalization at work. For the reaction is an adaptation to relevant aspects of the environment, and the same response serves to answer widely varying stimuli. In our own behaviour habit itself is a generalized response to situations; but there is now a reflective element present, which recognizes the situations to which we respond with a behaviour pattern already determined, as recurrences of the same type of situation; that is to say as abstractly identical, the abstraction being in terms of what is relevant to our intention.

In reflection, however, the intention is negative, or theoretical. From this certain consequences follow. First, the primary 'given' is the memory of a completed act. It can therefore be apprehended in terms of a distinction between means and end, for it is only in action that the end remains indeterminate. Second, since the given is determinate, while action always refers to the future, the distinction between act and event is irrelevant; and in the abstraction from action which constitutes the reflective intention, the given appears as a series of events constituting the unity of a process. The end is no longer intended; it merely constitutes the last event in the process isolated in attention, though the ground of this isolation is the fact that it *was* intended. In general then, the past, as the object of reflection, is given as a system of processes each of which consists of a series of events. Third, these processes and the events which constitute them are, in actuality, completely determinate; but for reflection they are only partially determined. The reason for this is that in action attention is governed by a practical intention, and only so much is noticed as is required for the purpose in hand; and for normal activities the determination is predominantly visual. In buying or selling, for example, one shilling is identical with another for all practical purposes; and the differences between different issues of the coinage go unnoticed. When, therefore, a theoretical intention replaces the practical, the given for thought is relatively indeterminate, and the activity of reflection is concerned to achieve a theoretically more adequate determination of this primary representation. The use of the term 'representation' in this connexion is literal. The elements of knowledge in action are 'presentations'. In reflection they are remembered and so become representative of the original presentation in action.

We have seen that any theoretical intention, being negative, cannot determine an end, and so a means to that end. Instead of an end it has an ideal; and instead of a means it has a method of procedure. Truth, for example, is in this sense an ideal. An ideal might be defined as a negative end; as the bare form of an end. For it can be defined only negatively in relation to a starting-point. Truth, for instance, might be defined as the completely adequate determination of the object; yet what this might be we cannot tell; since if we could we should already possess it and reflective activity would be both unnecessary and impossible. The definition has, however, a negative relation to our present knowledge: that is to say it expresses a recognition of its inadequacy and so of our ignorance. In this way it defines a method of procedure from the inadequate given towards its fuller determination by thought.

There are, however, two directions in which a fuller determination of data can be sought. The relative indeterminateness of a representation can be made more adequate either by generalization or by particularization. The terms 'general' (or 'universal') and 'particular', it should be noted, are logical correlatives. Neither the one nor the other has any reference to existence. Both refer to representations, and so to the theoretical activities which concern the production of adequate representations of the existent. What exists is the concrete individual, from which both the universal and the particular are ideal abstractions. To talk of a concrete universal is to confuse idea and existence; but it would be precisely the same error if we were to refer to the concrete particular. The concrete individual is given only in practical experience: in reflection we may limit our attention either to its particularity alone or only to its universal aspect. For purposes of cognition, therefore, we may either particularize a representation or universalize it. We cannot, however, do both at once. For that, as Kant rightly said, we should require an intellectual intuition; which would mean a reflective activity which should determine an object in contrary directions at the same time.

To particularize a representation is more than to fill in the detail which has been left out of account for practical purposes.

It is to complete the representation for the expression of the uniqueness of what is represented. For this purpose the elements discriminable in the representation must constitute a self-contained unity. Each element must refer to all the others, and nothing must refer the Subject beyond the representation. In other words, the representation must be so constituted that it holds the attention within itself, and so isolates itself from all external reference. So far as this can be achieved, the object is represented as an unconditioned whole, a unity in its own right, and therefore unique. Such a representation can only be produced as an image for intuition; and its production is the work of artistry. This is, of course, the *ideal* of particularization; and we particularize a representation when we develop it in the direction of such an ideal.

To generalize is to develop a representation in the opposite direction, so that what is represented appears not as unique but as constituted by its external relations. The process is one of analytical reduction. It is the 'negative' aspect of taking something to pieces and so reducing it to the elements of which it is composed. If I isolate any element in attention from the others with which, in actuality, it is conjoined, it ceases to have any necessary location either spatial or temporal. It might be anywhere or at any time. So abstracted, as a relationless element, it is a general idea. The blue of the sky becomes when isolated simply blue, which might occur as an element in any other visual context, actual or imaginary. I can generalize all the elements which make up a representation in this way. I have merely to exclude from consideration their relation to one another. On the other hand I can eliminate the elements and attend only to their relations in the representation, and so produce a representation which is purely schematic. This 'form' or 'schema of relations' is also general in the sense that other elements could be arranged in these relations. The pattern can again be analysed into the elementary relations of which it is composed, and which could be recombined in different ways to provide other relational patterns. The ideal of this type of reflective process is a complete generality—the idea of an infinite multiplicity of unit elements which can be related in an infinite number of different ways. It is essential to this ideal that all the elements should be represented as identical; since only in this way can all necessary connexion between them, and so all particularization, be eliminated. This, again, is an ideal which cannot be attained. Generalization is a process which moves in this direction. Generality and particularity are therefore polar opposites; and any representation is more or less general; less or more particular. If we call the completely general the pure concept and the completely particular the pure intuition, then any representation is more or less conceptual and less or more intuitional; and of course we can attend either to the conceptual or to the intuitional aspect of a representation to the exclusion of the other. Thus just as the artistic method of representation seeks the completely particular, so the ideal of science is a complete generality. Both are abstract; the concrete individual which is represented is both constituted by its relations to the rest of the real, and is a whole in its own right.

We shall return to this topic in the next chapter. In the meantime we must consider finally the derivation of theoretical from practical activity, in order to show how the standpoint of the 'I do' overcomes the dualism of thought and action which the theoretical standpoint makes inevitable. We should be clear first of all about the ground of discrimination between theoretical and practical from the standpoint of the Agent. It is not a distinction between material and mental entities or processes. In reflection, where the Self is subject and everything else, including its own past, is object, this distinction between material and non-material aspects can be made by selective attention. In action, however, the distinction is matter of intention; and the ground of distinction is the difference between a theoretical and a practical intention. A practical activity is one which intends a modification of the Other; a theoretical intention is one which intends a modification in the representation of the Other. In either case the *means* to the realization of the intention may involve a modification of the Other. The experiments which a scientist makes in his laboratory, and which involve the devising, erecting and manipulation of apparatus, are elements in a theoretical activity. The thinking out—the calculating and planning—which a builder undertakes before he starts to erect a factory are elements in a practical activity. Whether what I do involves moving things about or not is immaterial.

Now a practical intention is positive, while a theoretical intention is negative. Action, we have seen, involves knowledge as its negative aspect. The carrying out of a practical intention therefore involves a development of knowledge—or if you will, a continuous modification in the representation of the Other—as its negative aspect. This indeed is the source of that primary knowledge which comes unsought with the growth of experience. At every point in a practical activity there is a recognition of alternative possibilities and a choice, in action, of one of these. At certain points new possibilities are apprehended which are relevant to the attaining of the objective and so may involve a modification of the immediate intention. But this continuous modification of the representation in action is not itself intended: it is only the negative aspect of a practical activity—the 'attentional' aspect, we might say, of an intention which passes beyond the representation of a thing to terminate in the thing itself. A theoretical intention is then an intention which terminates in an idea, and does not pass beyond it. It is a limitation of practical activity. It intends a determination of our idea of the world without going beyond this to a determination of the world itself. For this reason the results of theoretical activity have a reference beyond themselves. For any development of knowledge makes possible a modification of action which was not possible without it, whether such a modification is intended or not. The extension of knowledge always extends the range of possibility for action. We noticed earlier that 'action' was an inclusive and 'thought' an exclusive concept. We may now say that in the same sense a practical intention is an inclusive and a theoretical intention an exclusive intention. Practical activity includes theoretical activity, of necessity, in its constitution. Theoretical activity excludes practical activity from its intention, though not necessarily from the means to the realization of its intention. Consequently its results are meaningless in themselves, and require a reference to action to give them meaning. They can be valid or invalid through a reference to the validity or invalidity of the practical activity which they suggest.

It remains only to indicate how, if the practical is primary, a theoretical activity can establish itself and even become dominant. To understand this, we should start from a practical activity in which movement and knowledge are continuously fused. We might choose, as our example, the case of a skilled carpenter producing a plane face on a piece of rough wood with a chisel. To exclude as far as possible anticipatory awareness we may assume that he has to do this in the dark, and so by tactual perception alone. The wood is felt throughout as a resistance at the cutting edge of the chisel; and the carpenter's skill is shown in a continuous modification of the amount and direction of the pressure he exerts in response to slight variations in the resistance. If he were teaching a tyro to do this he would no doubt instruct him to avoid any jerky movement and keep up an even pressure upon the chisel. This implies a practical assumption that the resistance of the timber is a continuant factor which does not alter; yet the action proceeds as an attentive expectation of and response to variations in the resistance as they arise. This is the typical pattern of rational activity. It proceeds on the assumption that the future will be as the past—for this alone provides a basis for the automatism of habit upon which all skill must be based. At the same time it expects that this will not be completely the case; and concentrates attention expectantly to meet actual variations from the pattern of continuance that is presupposed.

It is only by assuming abnormally simplified conditions, however, that we can isolate instances where movement and knowledge are so continuously complementary. Even in these, careful study will bring to light a rhythm of attention which swings between the awareness of the Other and the movement of the Agent. In normal experience, and especially when the range of anticipation is enlarged, the amplitude of this rhythm is increased. Consider an artist painting a picture. He alternately puts colour on the canvas and stands back to observe the effect; and this goes on until he can find no more to do and the picture is finished. While he is actually painting, of course, he sees what he is doing, and feels movement and resistance just as the carpenter does. But this looking and feeling is not enough. He must stand back and contemplate what he has done, to see it as a whole, before he does more. These contemplative moments are part of the practical business of producing his picture. The succession of positive and negative phases, of movement and of reflection, is so characteristic of the personal life that it would be well to have a name for it. We shall refer to it whenever we meet it as 'the rhythm of withdrawal and return'.

In most practical activities, the withdrawal into reflection is forced upon us because we meet unforeseen difficulties. We have to stop what we are doing and consider the next step. It may be that alternative procedures present themselves, between which we must choose, and the relative advantages and disadvantages of these must be considered. It may be that the means we are using fail to produce the expected result; and we have to think out a new method of procedure and start afresh. In all such cases the periods we spend in reflection and consideration fall within a dominant practical purpose, and are negative moments in the realization of a practical intention. We may notice here that the relative time spent in action and in reflection is of no theoretical importance. Many actions involve little reflection and much practical activity; others require much careful planning and then perhaps a single decisive act. Many would have been accomplished more speedily and more successfully if longer time had been spent in considering each step in advance.

We have been considering activities in which a definite and

fairly clearly defined end is in view. But many of our activities are not of this kind. Others consist in exploiting such means of action as we possess. These originate rather in a consideration of our resources and the possible activities in which they may be employed. In such cases the ends are, in a sense, dictated by the means. But the important point in this is that just as the same end may be attained by various means, so the same means may serve the attainment of various ends. Because of this it is possible to accumulate power—that is, the means of attaining our ends—without deciding in advance between the alternative purposes to which the power shall be put when we have got it. The accumulation of wealth is a case in point, since the richer I am the more alternative possibilities of action I possess. In such activity, the ultimate end remains undefined, and the intention terminates in the means, over long periods of time in many cases. Indeed, since the use of the power which is being accumulated may be postponed indefinitely, the pursuit of power may become, for a particular agent, an end in itself, however irrational and even meaningless such an intention may be. For power of any sort has meaning only in reference to an end beyond itself to which it is the means.

The intention here is still practical. But clearly it need not be. The reflective moment in a practical activity is itself concerned with the means to the realization of a practical end; and in many cases the knowledge it achieves can be applied in different activities than the one for which it was originally intended. Knowledge indeed is power in a special sense, and any increase in knowledge is an increase in power; since knowledge is actually a dimension of action, and without it an increase in material resources is nugatory. Consequently, the generalization of knowledge, as the negative aspect of action, makes possible an activity which intends the accumulation of knowledge, without any defined reference to the practical intentions which it makes possible; and so without reference to its application in action. The moment of withdrawal into reflection may be prolonged indefinitely, and the operative intention will then be a theoretical intention, with no specific reference to any practical intention to which it is the means. So knowledge may become an end in itself; even though this too is irrational and meaningless. For in the absence of all reference to the practical reflection becomes phantastic, incapable of either truth or falsity.

This then is one way in which it can be shown that though when we start from the primacy of the theoretical we can find no way to the possibility of action, yet when we start from the 'I do', the possibility of reflection is no mystery; and the dualism of mind and matter is overcome.

CHAPTER NINE

Modes of Reflection

We have seen how the activities of reflection are derived from action by a limitation of attention to its negative dimension; and how, in this manner, a purely reflective intention can emerge. We may summarize this, in terms of the form of the personal, in the following way. The unity of movement and knowledge in action makes the movement intentional. If now we isolate the negative aspect, it appears as the intention which informs the movement. Intention, in its turn, must reveal the negative aspect which it contains. This we call 'attention'. The negative intention which constitutes a theoretical activity is then a limitation of intention to its own negative aspect; it is an intentional attending to what has been given in action.

We must now consider the processes of reflection themselves, and in particular the manner in which they refer to action. Reflective activities we have defined as such doings of the Agent as terminate in ideas. We may now make this definition more complete by reference to the reflective intention. They are activities which intend the improvement of knowledge. Since knowledge is primarily a dimension of action, this limited and negative intention has an implied reference to practical intention, the improvement of action itself. So long, however, as the activity is governed by a negative intention, this reference remains implicit and indeterminate; and the reflective activity is in this sense undertaken for its own sake; that is to say, with no determinate reference to its practical application. This does not mean however, that it makes no difference to practical activity. Any modification of knowledge, since it is an agent's knowledge, necessarily involves a modification of his practical activity, whether this is intended or not. We clearly cannot change our ideas of the world in which we act without in some way modifying our way of acting. Even if we devote our lives to the pursuit of knowledge for its own sake, that is in itself a modification of our way of living. It involves a practical, and not merely a theoretical choice. It has the effect, however, of inverting the positive and negative aspects of action; so that practical activities become elements in a theoretical way of life; subordinated to a negative intention.

All reflective activities involve representation. We have already seen that perceptual activities other than tactual, are anticipatory, and so involve the formation of an image which is referred to a future contact. The general principle is that any reference to past or future involves a present representation. Now a representation is a symbol: that is to say, it is something present which takes the place of what is absent and is considered not for itself but for its reference to another. Since reflection is a withdrawal from action, it is a withdrawal from the immediate experience of the Other; because only in action can the Other be immediately perceived. From this we must conclude that all reflection involves a withdrawal into the Self; a self-isolation from the Other: and that all reflective activity is symbolic. For not only are the elements present to the Self symbolic representations of what is not present; but the activities of the Self upon them are symbolic activities, or activities of representation. As negative activities they refer to and have meaning only in their reference to the positive activities of practical life.

There is one aspect of this symbolic activity which is of special importance for our immediate theme. We have already noticed that all activities of reflection tend towards practical embodiment, and are prevented from doing so by activities which oppose, or inhibit them, so that the energy expended remains potential, within the Self. There is, however, no necessity that this inhibition of movement should be complete, or indeed that it should be maintained at all. For we have disposed of the dualism of mind and matter; and must beware of any tendency to construe the distinction between practical and theoretical activity in terms of this dualism. The distinction between practical and theoretical is not matter of fact, but matter of intention. Provided the intention remains negative, it matters nothing whether the bodily movements which are involved are externalized and made open to observation or not. If I use words as my symbols in reflection, it makes no difference to the nature of my activity whether I speak them aloud, or conceal them, hearing them only 'in my mind'. For whether uttered or not, they are symbols; and indeed, in this case they are images; at least if they are heard at all, 'externally' or 'internally'. What is essential is that any externalizations which are essential to the activity of reflection should be symbolic; they must have their meaning not in themselves but through a reference to something else. If, for example, we wish to study the geometrical properties of the circle, most of us will find it necessary to draw circles on paper and study these. But the figures we draw need only be approximately circular; for they are symbolic representations, and not themselves the proper objects of our thought. The same is true of the most fully externalized expressions of reflective activity, such as a dramatic performance on the stage. The movements of the actors are actual movements, yet the whole play is essentially a representation. It may be photographed and presented on the screen of a cinema; or it may be described in print and visualized more or less successfully by the reader. Yet it remains, in all these modes, the same play. We call such externalizations of a reflective activity 'expressions' and the process of producing them an 'activity of expression', or 'an expressive activity'. Now an activity of reflection is never complete until it is expressed. Most of our reflective activity finds its expression in words, either spoken or written. This is the end towards which it moves, and until it is expressed it remains incomplete. For reflective activities, like practical activities, may be broken off before their intention is fully realized. Every reflective activity is therefore an activity of expression, which is completed only by an external embodiment. Whatever precedes the external expression is a preparation for it. Sometimes the expression can be carried through to a point at which the external embodiment involves no modification of its essential meaning. But this is rare. Every student knows from experience how much of illusion lurks in the belief that his problem has been completely thought through and resolved before he has set anything out in writing. Quite apart from this, however, the incompleteness of the theoretical activity until it is externalized lies specially in this, that only so can it gain reality by becoming a deed, and take its place in history as an act. Publication is essential to the realization of reflection; and we do well to be sceptical of all 'mute, inglorious Miltons'.

A complete account of the modes of reflection is impossible at this stage, and even the reasons we can offer for our conclusions are incomplete. For the relations of persons are constitutive for the personal; and we are limiting our attention for the present to the Agent in isolation. One effect of this limitation is that we must treat the end of reflective activity as its *expression*, and not as its *communication*. Expression, indeed, is the negative aspect of communication, and so is included in and derivative from communication. All expression implies, even when it does not intend, a sharing of experience; to express ourselves to nobody is pointless, and ultimately meaningless. But this is only one aspect of a more fundamental incompleteness to which our present standpoint limits us. Many reflective activities, and these the primary and basic types, themselves refer to and symbolize practical activities which are common and co-operative, so that they are meaningless apart from the relation of persons. They may even require a common activity for their expression. We might instance the celebration of a golden wedding.

We must distinguish three modes of reflection. In their purest expression—by which I mean when they are determined by a purely reflective intention—they are religion, art and science. All of them, however, since they are necessarily derived from practical experience, and refer symbolically to action, have intermediate forms in which the reference to practical experience is more specific or more limited. Of these three modes, the religious is the primary one, from which the other two are derived by limitation of attention. Nevertheless we shall have to leave this mode undiscussed, because its reference is always and essentially to persons in relation. Even art and science we shall not discuss as such, but only in terms of the two modes of reflection of which they are the pure forms. To the pure forms themselves we shall have to return at a later stage.

To distinguish these two modes of solitary reflection we must raise a question which has been postponed until now. How is the unit of action—an individual act—to be defined? From the standpoint of the Agent, the Real is a complex of continuous change, in which he distinguishes between action and happening, and within each category he further distinguishes individual units, whether acts or events. These individual occurrences are temporally discriminated. They have a beginning and an end. Whatever changes connect the beginning with the end are parts of the one occurrence; yet the whole occurrence is itself part of a system of occurrences, and necessarily related to what preceded and to what follows it. What then distinguishes one occurrence from the general process of occurrence of which it is a part?

So far as events are concerned, as distinct from actions, the discrimination is arbitrary. The choice of a unit is determined by the observer to suit his own purpose. So far as his purposes are determinate, the choice of a unit is at least partly determinate: but this determination is relative to the agent. It is not purely objective. The more purely theoretical the intention, and therefore the more indeterminate the practical reference becomes, the freer is the selection of a unit. This is apt to be obscured by the fact that the major distinctions within the Other are already determined in action; and they are carried over into our reflective activities as already 'given'. We can, however, if it suits our theoretical purpose, disregard these distinctions, and discriminate the given in any way that is suitable.

This, however, is not the case when we are determining the unit of action. For though here again the discriminating factor is the intention of an agent, this intention is now constitutive of the action itself. Consequently an individual act has a beginning and an end of its own, and these are determined by the intention which constitutes it an act. It begins when it is initiated, and ends when it is either completed or broken off. Its beginning and ending are intentional, not merely factual. Two comments, however, are necessary to avoid misunderstanding. Firstly, this does not imply that the unit of action is completely determinate; if only because intention is not itself determinate, but determines itself in process. What is, retrospectively, a single act, may therefore consist of a number of subsidiary acts. These subsidiary acts are themselves defined by subsidiary intentions which fall within a larger intention. This may happen either because an end which was determined from the beginning is accomplished in stages—the means to its achievement being progressively determined; or because the accomplishing of an original intention leads on to another, and so becomes a means to a more distant end which was not originally intended. Secondly, we should note that it is always possible to treat an act *as if* it were an event once it is complete; or even, if it is not my own act, while it is being performed. But this does not *make* it an event; it is only an incomplete or abstract representation which may be justified for certain purposes.

From this point of view we may define an act as the realizing of an intention. We have to remember, of course, that the intention itself may not be determined completely in advance: and that our actions often fail to realize their intention, and are then broken off, either voluntarily or of necessity. But since we are concerned now with reflective activity, we may ignore these points and consider only actions which are completed successfully. In such cases the intention is determinate and is realized. Only the completed act is a unit for reflective consideration.

If we so consider it, we realize that the beginning and the end of an act are defined by the agent's *feeling*; the former by a negative and the latter by a positive feeling. We may describe the one as a feeling of dissatisfaction, and the other as a feeling of satisfaction. Feeling is necessary to provide a motive for action; because the mere awareness of a situation, however clearly it determines the object as such and such, as matter of fact, provides no ground for action. Equally, a mere feeling, unrelated to an awareness of the situation as matter of fact, could not issue in action, but at most in a reaction to stimulus. If the feeling is not *referred* to the situation it cannot provide a motive. If, for example, I feel afraid, my fear characterizes the situation in which I find myself as dangerous, and normally the reference of the feeling is specific. I discover that my retreat has been cut off by the tide, or that there is a bull in the field I am crossing. My fear may be mistaken, or it may be correct. If there is no danger, my fear characterizes the situation falsely; if there is, then I am right in feeling afraid. Such a recognition of danger, through the reference of feeling to a situation, initiates an action. In general, a feeling of dissatisfaction characterizes a situation as unsatisfactory; and so provides a motive for initiating an act to change it; while the successful removal of the unsatisfactoriness by action terminates the action. For when the result of the acting is felt to be satisfactory there is no more to be done. The action is complete; and the agent withdraws from action into reflection.

Feeling, then, when referred to an object, is valuation; and the most general discrimination in valuation is the acceptance or rejection of a possibility in action. We have seen that action is choice; it implies the realization of one of a number of possibles and the negation of the others. From this we inferred that a distinction between right and wrong was inherent in the nature of action. We can now particularize this point more fully. The reflective element in action has a double function. It discriminates the Other as a set of possibilities of action; and it also selects one of these possibilities for realization in action. At its lower limit this selection is simply a concentration of attention upon one possibility to the exclusion of the others. Thus we find again, by another approach, that attention is the negative aspect of intention. Now since action is primary, our primary knowledge of the world contains both of these moments—apprehension and valuation—in a unity. The world is known primarily as a system of possibilities of action; and without valuation action is impossible; and consequently, knowledge, which is its negative dimension, is also impossible. If now we withdraw from action, and so from all practical intention, we abstract from the activity of practical valuation. The world is then apprehended, in terms of this abstraction, as an existent manifold of events. This manifold constitutes the given for a mode of reflective activity which seeks to understand the world as matter of fact, and this activity excludes any positive valuation.

We must not forget, however, that it cannot exclude a negative valuation. Reflective activity is still something that we do; and is therefore intentional. This reflective intention is, we have seen, a negative intention; it is the intention to attend. But attention is selective. It is impossible simply to attend to all that is there; and the activity of attending is itself a choosing between alternatives. In the result, the understanding we reach, the conclusions we obtain, depend on what, in the given, we attend to; and exclude from their scope what was excluded from attention. Moreover, this activity of attention must have a motive, and so must imply a valuation of the given from the point of view of what is relevant and irrelevant for our purpose. If the intention is purely theoretical, that is to say, if the reference to action is indeterminate, then the ground of valuation must itself be negative. It must, that is to say, be the continuation of a direction of attention which was originally established in action; and which can be expressed in a methodological rule. It is a corollary of this that reflective activity of this type must issue, not in a single science of the given, but in a set of independent sciences, each constituted by the selectivity of its own direction of attention.

The subjective correlate of this exclusion of practical valuation is the suppression of feeling in favour of sensory discrimination. For what is intended is now a determination of fact. Whether the situation disclosed is satisfactory or unsatisfactory falls outside the intention, and is not attended to. The ideal of this mode of reflection is therefore a pure activity of thought which is unaffected by feeling; which is cool, passionless and completely disinterested, seeking truth for its own sake, with no eye to any practical advantage for the seeker or for anyone else. In our tradition this type of passionless reflection has been identified with reason. The identification is quite arbitrary and groundless. Its source lies in the persistent influence of the Stoic tradition with its characteristic dualism between Reason and the Passions—a distinction originally instituted to support a particular ethical theory. This mode of reflection is of course rational, since it is a mode of personal activity, and reason is the *differentia* of the personal. But it has no unique claim to rationality, and it is indeed not the primary expression of reason. The proper term to describe it is not 'rational' but 'intellectual'; and I propose therefore to refer to it hereafter as the intellectual mode of reflective activity.

We have seen that in reflection any complete act, since it is apprehended as a whole, must be analysed into an end, and a means to that end. This distinction between 'means' and 'end' is clearly not mere matter of fact. It refers to the valuation which determines the action. The end is that in the action which is valued for its own sake, that in which the intention terminates, and in which the agent comes to rest and is satisfied. The means, on the other hand, is everything in the action which is valued not for its own sake. The means is, of course, chosen in action, and this involves valuation. But because the intention passes beyond it and does not rest in it, its valuation is derivative from the end, and it has no value for the agent in itself. The end is enjoyed—it has an intrinsic value for the agent—but not the means. The means is discriminated, and chosen, from amongst alternatives; but only for the end, and not for itself. Now in an intellectual mode of reflection, because there is a suppression of feeling and an abstraction from practical valuation, the distinction between means and end disappears, and only a succession of occurrences remains. Since these are no longer referred to an agent, they appear as a succession of events in time, necessarily related, but with no end in which the succession terminates. The process is continued into its consequences *ad infinitum*. But since all reflection refers to action, a purely intellectual intention must have an indeterminate reference. This reference can become determinate, and so enter into action as its negative dimension, only through the determination of an end by a practical intention. In other words, intellectual knowledge, as knowledge of matter of fact, becomes in action knowledge of the means of realizing a practical intention. For all that is so known is in itself valueless; and in action it can be valued only negatively, as means to an end which it does not itself determine. From the standpoint of the Agent, then, intellectual reflection is an activity which intends an improvement of our knowledge of the world as means to our ends. We may express this succinctly by saying that intellectual knowledge is knowledge of the World-as-means. It is therefore the negative mode of reflection.

The positive mode of reflection is an activity of reflective valuation. Since it is an activity of valuation, it is primarily an activity of feeling; but since feeling must be referred to an object, and the object must be determined as matter of fact, reflective valuation contains within it, as its negative aspect, a perceptual discrimination of fact. Since it is a reflective activity, it abstracts from action, and its intention is a negative or theoretical intention. Its reference to action, that is to say, is indeterminate. Since its activity upon the given is an activity of feeling, we may distinguish it from the other mode of reflection by calling it the emotional mode.

Emotional reflection is the primary mode of reflective activity. It constitutes, indeed, the moment of withdrawal from action, in the realization of a practical intention. The Agent comes to rest when his purpose is accomplished and contemplates his achievement. So it is said in the story of the Creation in Genesis that 'God saw everything that He had made, and behold! it was very good'. This *theoria* or contemplation is the original reflective moment in the rhythm of withdrawal and return. It is essentially an enjoyment of what has been done and is now complete, and so a moment of evaluation. If we abstract from the valuation, and concentrate attention upon its negative aspect, we have the idea of pure sense perception, as the ideal dividing line between action and reflection. It is strictly ideal, for a pure receptivity is impossible. Pure sense-perception can only occur as the starting point of a reflective activity which is either emotional or intellectual.

As an enjoyment of what has been done, this original reflective valuation abstracts from the means and concentrates attention on the ends of action. Now if we abstract wholly from action, and bring this contemplation under a fully reflective intention, it must become an activity which seeks to determine intrinsic value. In this mode of reflection, therefore, whatever is selected in attention is considered as an end in itself; as existing for itself, and not as a means to anything beyond it; as there to be enjoyed, not used. Consequently we may say of the emotional mode of reflection that it seeks to determine the world as an end in itself, or rather as a manifold of ends. As we called intellectual knowledge knowledge of the World-as-means, so we may describe emotional knowledge as knowledge of the World-as-end.

We must consider for a moment at this point the conception of 'motive' in action, and in particular its distinction from and its relation to 'intention'. The distinction between motive and intention is difficult, and indeed impossible, for any philosophy which accepts the primacy of the theoretical, and takes its stand upon the 'Cogito'. For the motives of our actions are not thought, but felt; and if we represent them as thought, they become indistinguishable from intentions. From the standpoint of the Agent, however, the distinction is both important and clear-cut. One aspect of the difference, from which we may begin, is that the motive of an action need not be conscious, while the intention must be. To talk of an unconscious motive makes sense; but 'an unconscious intention' is a contradiction in terms. The phrase could only signify 'an intention which is unintentional'. An action, in the sense in which we are using the term, is necessarily intentional. It is indeed the presence of intention which distinguishes it from activities which are non-rational, uninformed by knowledge. Now we have already found that if we abstract from the element of knowledge which constitutes action, we are left with a motive consciousness, whether at the level of feeling or of sense; and also that this motive consciousness, or rather this conscious behaviour falls within action as a negative aspect. Every action, then, has a motive. But it does not follow that the motive determines the action, or that the agent is conscious of his motive; or if he is somehow aware of it, that he attends to it. What determines an action is its intention; but we shall be prepared to find that the motive of an action is contained within the intention as its negative aspect.

The term 'motive' signifies, in general, that which determines movement. Its scientific equivalent is 'energy'. But its characteristic use is limited to directed movements; to movements which have a purposive character. In organic behaviour, therefore, motive is that which accounts for the release of potential energy in response to a stimulus. Where we suppose consciousness to be involved—say, as a feeling of fear—then this feeling is the motive of the reaction, since it accounts for the direction in which energy is expended in movement. Because the reaction is defensive, that is to say, an avoidance of danger, we require a motive to account for its purposive character. But we do not suppose, or at least we have no reason to suppose, that any cognition is involved. The organism does not *know* that it is in danger, or what the danger is. Consequently its response to stimulus has a motive, but no intention; and this motive awareness accounts for the reaction, and determines its character.

In the case of agents, however, motives do not determine action. Nevertheless, all action contains necessarily an element of reaction to stimulus, without which it would be impossible. We call this habit; and the system of habits in an individual agent we call his character. The reason, we have seen, for distinguishing personal habits from organic responses to stimuli, is that they are not innate but have to be learned. They are formed in action, and they are subject to deliberate modification and reformation. But once formed, and while they persist, they operate through an automatic or semi-automatic response to recurrent stimuli; though this is always complicated by the presence of cognition. In so far then as an agent acts habitually, he acts from a motive, but not with intention. But in normal action these motived responses are aspects of an activity which *is* intentional; and because attention is concentrated upon the objective, the motives of these habitual aspects of action normally remain unconscious, unless they are brought into consciousness by reflection.

In all conscious behaviour then, the motive is a feeling, which governs the expenditure of energy by selecting its direction. This control includes the negative phase—the inhibition of movement. The basic differentiation of feeling is into positive and negative forms, which determine movements of attraction and of repulsion respectively. We must therefore distinguish between positive and negative motivation; the positive controlling the activities which constitute the life-process of an organism, the negative being defensive. Feeling, we have seen, is differentiated both quantitatively and qualitatively, and its distinguishable modes are combined in very complex patterns; each of which is more or less positive or negative according to the preponderance of positive or negative elements in it. Sensory consciousness, when it is present, rests upon and is itself controlled by feeling, which directs energy to the formation of images; and these images in turn modify feeling. Mere sensation, unassociated with feeling, is an impossibility; and if it were possible it could not of itself determine a reaction. The function of sensation in activity is to make possible a wider range and a finer discrimination of possible reactions, in particular by anticipation. But the selection of the direction of response remains the function of feeling.

Now in personal activity, all this organic activity falls within action, and is therefore raised to the level of intention. With the distinction between Self and Other, both images and feelings are referred to the Other, and action is determined by knowledge. This knowledge has two aspects, a determination of the Other as matter of fact in relation to action, and so an apprehension of the possibilities open to the Agent; and a valuation of these possibilities in action, and so the determination of an intention. These two aspects of knowledge are of course not separable in fact, but only distinguishable by thought. The discrimination of the Other—as support for and resistance to action—is perception; the valuation of alternatives is matter of feeling.

When we refer to the motive of an action, in distinction from its intention, what we have in mind is the constellation of feeling in which it originates. Any state of feeling has a tendency to express itself in action; and would do so unless controlled by intention. Under abnormal conditions we do find instances of behaviour which escape from intentional control and are completely determined by their motives. When a person loses his temper, or is overwhelmed by passion or falls into a panic this is what happens. Then, as we say, a man 'becomes irresponsible', or 'loses his self-control', or 'acts purely on impulse'. In such circumstances the distinction between motive and intention is particularly clear. We must not forget, however, that the patterns of feeling which constitute our motives are themselves the product of an intentional experience; and that they continue responses to the environment which have been deliberately established in the past. The impulsive activities of an agent are therefore normally 'in character'; though they are not determined by a present intention. A person's character is the persistent system of motives from which he acts under normal conditions; and when we predict what he is likely to do in given conditions from a knowledge of his character, we abstract from intention, and suppose that his motives will determine his actions. Motive, we may then say, is the continuant element in action; it determines the general direction of an agent's behaviour, while the particular actions he performs are determined by the particular intentions he forms from moment to moment in terms of his discrimination and valuation of his situation as he knows it. Nor is there any reason, in principle, why he should not act intentionally in complete opposition to his momentary inclination; for inclination is simply the tendency for feeling to realize itself in action, which is normally subject to intentional control.

We may now return to our consideration of the two modes of reflection which are open to the solitary agent. Of the intellectual mode we need say little, because philosophy has been so largely concerned with it, and most of what we should have to say is already familiar. It is, we have said, a determination of the World-as-means. It expresses itself therefore in a generalized representation of the world as matter of fact; in the production of formulae which express the recurrent patterns of continuance in experience. When carried on systematically for its own sake, it is science. In reference to action it provides an improvement in our technical knowledge, in particular by the great extension of anticipation which it makes possible. By means of systematic intellectual reflection, and its expression in generalized information, we discover increasingly what we may count on, with greater or less probability, as the support for our actions, or as the means to the realization of our intentions.

The emotional mode of reflection is less familiar because more neglected by modern philosophy. Like the intellectual mode, it has its starting point in sense-perception, and therefore, abstracting from action, in representation. As an activity of reflection, however, it moves towards a greater particularization of the representation; and by this it expresses a valuation of what is represented as an end in itself.

Whatever is felt to be satisfactory is enjoyed for its own sake. This activity of enjoyment is contemplation. Its ideal is 'the perfect', that which could only be changed for the worse. Any practical activity in relation to what is felt to be valuable in itself must therefore be negative; the intention must be to keep it as it is, to preserve it from change; to make it, as Thucydides said, a κτῆμα ἐς ἀεί—a possession for ever, a permanent possibility of enjoyment. Contemplation itself, however, is an activity of reflection, and is necessarily directed upon a representation. What is past cannot be experienced in action; it can only be represented in reflection, and since it is now represented as an end—in its being for itself—it can only be represented through an image, that is to say, through a sensuous particularization of its representation. Again, since the activity is reflective, its intention is receptive, and the spontaneity involved in it is a means to this end. It is an activity of expression for the sake of contemplation; the production of an adequate image as a symbol of that to which it refers. The activity of emotional reflection, then, systematically pursued for its own sake, is pure art, just as the intellectual is pure science.

Both these modes of reflection are activities of knowing. This will be accepted without question in the case of science; but not, perhaps, in the case of art. Yet, if one of the two is to be refused the title of knowledge—and I can see no reason for such a discrimination—it is art that has the better claim. For whatever concerns us merely as means to an end is never apprehended for itself, but only in relation to something else. Our interest is only in those properties which make it useful to us, and these are general properties which it shares with other things. They are often referred to as causal properties. Intellectual reflection, as knowledge of the World-as-means, aims at knowing everything in general but nothing in particular. In this mode we come to know a great deal about things without knowing *them*. It is only when our interest, and so our valuation, comes to rest in something for itself, only when something becomes for us an end-in-itself, that we seek to know it for itself, instead of making generalizations from it. This knowledge of things as they are in themselves is the intention of contemplation. When something of which we have been aware attracts our attention so that we stop to contemplate it, we really see it for the first time. We isolate it from its surroundings. Our eyes search it systematically in detail, and discover a hundred things in it that we had overlooked, and these are held together in their intrinsic and particular relations to one another and to the whole which they constitute. The visual image ceases to be merely schematic and moves towards completeness. This, surely, is the way in which we *know* an object; the way in which we know a piece of country which we love because our home is there in contrast to the knowledge we acquire about other countries which we have never visited. We must add, what seems conclusive in this matter, that when we know anything at all in this contemplative fashion, we can derive from it at will a catalogue of its properties. But the opposite is not true. No intellectual description of an object, however complete and scientific, can ever amount to, or take the place of a contemplative knowledge of the thing itself. The intellectual mode of reflection is derivative from the emotional, and is contained within it. We can indeed trace the process of derivation in the history of Greek philosophy, and see, for example, how a theory of forms—aesthetically contemplated—is the source of a theory of universals. If we were to use the customary distinction between subjective and objective here, we should have to say that scientific knowledge is more subjective than artistic knowledge; and that the nearer it approximates to its ideal of a pure generality, the more subjective it becomes.

This discrimination of the object in contemplation is not intellectual. For it is not analytical, and it does not generalize. The elements discriminated remain essentially within the whole and there is no reference beyond the whole. They are not apprehended as instances of a concept. The process of contemplation is a discriminating valuation; a particularizing of the satisfactoriness of the object as a unity in itself, and for its own sake. It is, therefore, felt, and not analytically understood. The feeling, however, is objective, because the interest of the Subject is in the object itself, and in its particularity. An intellectual interest in an object is a subjective interest, and refers to the use-value of the object, that is to say, its value as a means to some agent's practical intentions, actual or possible. The satisfactoriness of the object in itself is apprehended through the feeling of satisfaction I experience, and the discrimination of the object in contemplation is achieved through a discrimination of this feeling. For this reason the activity of reflection is emotional and not intellectual; and its objective is to achieve an adequate and discriminating feeling for the object, and so an adequate, objective valuation of it.

If it is to achieve actuality, the emotional apprehension of an object must be expressed, and become independent of the subject. It must be published, and become matter of fact, even while it retains its symbolic character. There is an original relation between the feeling of satisfaction in perceptual experience, and aesthetic expression. Singing and dancing are probably its primary forms. The distinctive character of such expressions of emotion are rhythm, proportion, balance and harmony. The reason for this we have already touched upon. It is precisely these characters which make the representation a whole in itself, and confine the attention within it, so isolating it as a unity in its own right. The general effect we express by such terms as grace, beauty, loveliness and the like. They render the representation a satisfactory object of contemplation. What is so symbolized is that which has an intrinsic value, and is an end in itself; that which has in itself, as it were, a right to exist. Its contemplation refines our knowledge of the objective grounds for choosing, in action, to realize one possibility rather than another.

This is as far as we can carry the consideration of the two modes of individual reflection at the moment. We shall have to return to them later in a less egocentric context. There is, however, one final issue to which some reference should be made. All judgements of value, it is sometimes said, are simply emotive. They express merely our feelings, and cannot therefore be true or false. Only judgements of fact can constitute knowledge, since only these have an objective meaning which permits of verification. To this I must reply that such doctrine is itself a valuation and a false valuation at that. It expresses an exclusive over-valuation of intellectual reflection. That all valuation is the work of feeling I agree, and that its expression is an expression of feeling I have no doubt. But why 'merely'? Might I not as well say that an assertion of fact is 'merely' an expression of a thought that occurred in me? That logical thought is objective, while feeling is 'purely' subjective, is surely a dogma for which no rational ground can be offered. If our feelings are subjective because they occur in us, why not our thoughts which as surely occur to us? If our thoughts are objective because they refer to objects, then our feelings, which refer to objects in their own fashion, are objective also. If our thoughts are verified in action, so are our valuations. Is it not the case that our judgement that some experience which we seek will satisfy us is often falsified by the event? Both our feelings and our thoughts have their symbolic expressions; an assertion of fact which I make is an expression of my thought just as an assertion of value is an expression of my feeling. If it can be also a correct or incorrect description of an object, why may not the expression of my feeling for an object be a correct or an incorrect valuation of the object? And if an expression of feeling is emotive in the sense that it is an attempt to make other people feel as I do, is not the expression of what I think, in precisely the same sense, an effort to make other people think as I do? No relevant difference between the two modes of reflection is to be found unless it be this, that to verify a valuation I must commit myself in action by making it my end. Sometimes, indeed, I must stake my happiness, my reputation or even my life on the experiment; and if I find I was mistaken there may be no possibility of trying again.

CHAPTER TEN

The World as One Action

We must conclude our study of the Self as agent, by considering how, from this point of view, the unity of experience can be thought. But before doing this I should like to remind my readers of the two limitations to which this whole study is subject; for if these are forgotten, misunderstanding is liable to follow. The first is the limitation of purpose. No attempt has been made to achieve a systematic comprehensiveness. The design has been to justify, as the philosophical need of the present time, the substitution of a practical for a theoretical point of view; and, thereafter, to indicate, in regard to a few selected issues, the modification of theory which seems to be required. None of these issues has been considered with the methodical thoroughness which their separate importance demands, nor has there been any pretension to anticipate and answer the many objections to which such conclusions as have been reached are certainly open. Anyone who looks for a philosophical system, or demands a detailed and scholarly demonstration will be disappointed. Systematic scholarship is of the highest importance in philosophy; but it belongs to a later stage of the process which is here only initiated. For until we have familiarized ourselves with a new standpoint, and taken a few tentative bearings on the more obvious and outstanding landmarks, the attempt to construct in detail the map of a new landscape could only result in distortion and confusion. It is only the already sufficiently familiar that can be systematized and demonstrated, while the obvious objections which spring to our minds are apt to be grounded in the standpoint which it is proposed to abandon.

The second limitation is methodical. Our criticism of the tradition of modern philosophy was twofold; that it was theoretical, and that it was egocentric. In this first part of our study, we have sought to overcome the first of these defects only, by thinking from the standpoint of the Agent and not of the Subject. But we have retained the egocentric outlook; considering various aspects of our experience from the standpoint of the Agent in isolation. The result of this has been that some aspects, and these the most fundamental, have had to be omitted altogether. We have given no account of religion, of morality, of political society or of philosophy itself; for these aspects of our experience are grounded in our relations to one another. Indeed we were driven to recognize, in considering the implications of action, that action itself is impossible unless there is presupposed a plurality of agents in relation to one another in one field of operation. Consequently, any conclusion which we can reach at this point must be incomplete; and all that we have said so far must be held liable to modification and revision when later we seek to overcome the egocentric predicament to which we are still in bondage.

Within those limits there is a conclusion to be drawn concerning the unity of experience as it appears from the standpoint of the Agent. The only way in which we can conceive our experience as a whole is by thinking the world as one action. It will facilitate the exposition of this concept, however, if we first consider one of the reflective disciplines which we have hitherto left unexamined, and which, in its own way, underlies and encloses all the others. I refer to history. In distinguishing between two modes of reflective activity in the last chapter we were following an old tradition which distinguishes between the sciences and the arts. Philosophers have found it difficult to determine whether history should be classed as one or the other; and historians themselves have wavered between the two ideals, sometimes treating the writing of history as a form of imaginative literature and sometimes using a scientific procedure, so far as their subject matter would allow. Certain schools of philosophy, on the other hand, have insisted upon the intimate relation between history and philosophy and in some cases have gone so far as to identify the two.

The reason for this ambiguity and hesitation lies in the fact that history is concerned with action, and any attempt to determine its place among the reflective disciplines from a purely theoretical point of view involves itself in insuperable difficulties. We should expect, therefore, that the adoption of the Agent's point of view should resolve this ambiguity; and that its ability to do so should provide a justification of the new standpoint. History, then, is concerned with action, in the sense that the subject matter of the historian's reflection is the doings of men in the world. Here the distinction between 'action' and 'process', between 'what is done' and 'what happens', is of primary significance. What merely happens lies outside the historian's province. He is concerned with natural events and organic processes only in so far as they enter into the activities of human beings and play their part in setting the field for human decisions. This is indeed obvious when we attend to the historian's procedures; yet the influence of the philosophy of organism has tended to obscure it. The use of organic categories in general, and of the concept of evolution in particular, had a double effect. It stimulated a new interest in the study of history; and at the same time confused history with organic development. This confusion has had two interrelated consequences. On the one hand, the concept of history has been applied in general to all processes of natural development. We tend to describe any attempt to understand things by reference to their origin as 'historical', and to talk of the 'history' of the earth or the 'history' of a biological species. On the other hand, we tend to apply organic categories, and particularly the idea of evolution, in the field of history proper, and so to think of our human past as a determinate natural continuance which could not have been otherwise. Historians themselves have not been greatly affected by this confusion: their material is too recalcitrant. At most it has influenced their selection of data and their method of procedure to some extent. But it is responsible for a crop of philosophies of history and interpretations of history which have had important practical results, of which the most portentous is the communist movement. It is not the only one, however. The liberal faith in an inevitable progress has the same confusion at its source. To some extent this is a question of words. There is no serious objection to using the term 'history' with reference to natural processes; and we have seen that action necessarily contains natural processes as its negative aspect, so that an abstraction of these for relevant purposes is justifiable. No questions, however, are *merely* verbal; for the language we choose has its overtones and its suggestions. If I say that the battle of Waterloo happened in 1815, I may be tempted to ask what caused it; and in my answer, to treat human decisions and intentions as mere matter of fact. It will be safer to say that the battle *was fought* in 1815; for then language will itself suggest the proper historical questions, 'Who fought it?' and 'What were they fighting about?'

We must notice next the essential inclusiveness of history. Since knowledge is a dimension of action, no extension of knowledge can be without a practical consequence. Natural events, as such, do not enter into history. But the knowledge of them does; and even our speculations about the unknown add their quota to the determination of our intentions in action. Nature itself, we have seen, with all her events and processes, organic or inorganic, is an ideal abstraction. So far as natural events enter into human experience they modify human action, and so come within the scope of history. If it be urged that very much happens in the world of which we are ignorant, and that the world itself exists independently of us and of our knowledge, it must be admitted that this is the case, and that we know it to be the case. Yet our very ignorance is a negative element in the determination of our intentions; and the historian can only understand the actions of men in the past by recognizing their ignorance of much that is familiar today. History, therefore, is in this sense all-inclusive. The whole human past, with all the knowledge that informed it, with all the errors and illusions and misjudgements which distorted it, is matter of history; and there is no event, however seemingly remote from our practical interests, which may not turn out to be relevant to the historian's task. The sciences and the arts, philosophy and religion all have their histories; and these histories are not separate histories but parts of the one history which is the story of the doings of man on the earth. It is indeed one of the more important theoretical consequences of the practical standpoint that we should cease to look upon the sciences as independent 'bodies of truth' and learn to think of them as human performances, as things that men do.

This inclusive character history shares with philosophy. These two disciplines have, as it were, a common starting point; it is the whole of the past as entering into the determination of action. The history of philosophy is part of history; but it is also part of philosophy in a way that the history of a science is not a part of that science. For philosophy, like history, is one, and every new philosophy is a continuation of the one philosophy just as every new history of an age is a rewriting of the one history. The difference between the two is that while philosophical reflection generalizes, historical reflection particularizes. It is this refusal of generalization, this effort to represent the particularity of temporal sequence, which makes history seem, in some respects, to be art rather than science. Yet it does not, as an art does, express a reflective valuation: for it is concerned to represent matter of fact, and in this it stands closer to science. Unlike science, however, it does not seek to discover recurrent patterns which could form a basis for prediction. History, then, is neither an art nor a science, though it has certain affinities with both. How then are we to place it among the reflective activities of the Self?

To answer this question we must return to the moment of withdrawal from action. This is the negative moment in action, in which the Agent isolates himself from contact with the Other

—not, of course, in fact, but in intention—and so becomes the Subject in contemplation. The object of reflection is then what has been done, and so is determinate and continuant. This is, we have decided, the past. What represents the past for the Subject is the content of memory. Memory is the present representation of what has been known in action, as a contemporary whole. But though it is given as a whole, its representation is incomplete and inadequate. For memory contains only what was noticed by the agent; and this noticing has been determined selectively by a practical intention. Until the end is attained, until the moment of withdrawal, the Other is known only as means to an end, and what is noticed is therefore only so much as is relevant to its use as means. The immediate content of memory, therefore, is only so much as was adequate to the particular intention of an action; and this is completely inadequate to the reflective intention, which is theoretical.

The various ways in which memory is inadequate and unreliable as a knowledge of the past are well known to everyone from experience, and have been the subject of much psychological investigation. They need not detain us here. One or two points, however, deserve mention because they are pertinent to our immediate theme. First, we may notice that there is a reflective activity of remembering, when we make an effort to recall something we have experienced in the past. This effort serves to fix an event in memory; that is, to facilitate its subsequent recall; and the more often we recall a past experience the more readily available it becomes. But this fixing of an experience in memory is notoriously unreliable. The main reasons are that the activity of recall is an imaginative process, so that it is difficult to be sure that the recall is purely reproductive and not inventive. Moreover, what is actually remembered is usually fragmentary and demands imaginative completion. There is always apt to be an unconscious modification or idealization of the memory content in the deliberate effort to remember.

Secondly, the process of observation is itself an activity of memory. For contemplation takes time, and though the intention is to apprehend something as a unity in itself, the activity is a succession of observations which are fused together in a memory-synthesis. Add to this that visual perception of events is in principle always a perception of the past, since light takes time to travel from the object to the eye; and though for practical purposes this interval is negligible, it becomes theoretically important where the distances, as in astronomical observation, are sufficiently great. The anticipatory function of vision in action rests upon the assumption of continuance. But a particular event does not recur; what does recur is another event of the same type. Auditory perception, again, depends upon the speed of sound, which is much slower than that of light, so that allowance must be made for this at much lesser distances. In general, since the present is the point of action, it is only in tactual contact that our awareness of the Other is not a knowledge of the past.

Thirdly, the content of memory is relative to the position and the action of a particular agent. Under normal conditions at least we can remember only what we have ourselves experienced, that is to say only our own past. It is believed by some that nothing we have ever experienced is totally lost to memory; and the use by psychologists of techniques for the overcoming of amnesia provides impressive evidence for such a generalization. But even if this is true, there are still two points to be taken into account. The first is that it is rarely possible to be sure that we are really remembering and not inventing; and second, that even if this difficulty could be overcome, even if a particular agent could remember all he had ever experienced, and could be sure that his memory was completely trustworthy, the content of his memory would constitute only a tiny fragment of what there has been to experience. As a knowledge of the past it would amount to very little.

I have drawn attention to these characteristics to provide a background for the conclusion which specially concerns us. The inadequacy of memory as a knowledge of the past comes from the fact that no reflective activity is complete until it is expressed; and this expression must itself be independent of the continuing activity of the Self. This expressing of memory we call 'recording'; and when it is pursued systematically we speak of 'compiling records'. When it is important that we should remember something with precision, it is better not to trust our unaided memory, but to make a note of it. If we wish to be able, in the future, to recall our past experience and activities satisfactorily, we keep a diary. Such records, we know, must be made when the experiences to which they refer are still fresh in the memory if they are to be reliable. All such records are expressions of the activity of remembering; they are not so much substitutes for memory as memories published. For the records in themselves are mere symbols; and if I read in my diary I remember my past experience, with an exactness and a detail which would otherwise be impossible. But the recording of my experience has also the effect of making it public, in the sense that someone else can read what I have written. If this happens, my knowledge of my own past, which is the content of my memory, becomes his knowledge of my past. So my memories, through the record I make, become elements in a public memory, a knowledge of past experience which has become available to anyone who reads the record.

Now both the modes of reflection which we have examined, the intellectual and the emotional, depend upon the recording of personal experience. The scientist must record his observations and experiments with meticulous exactness, and he must have access to the records made by others. The artist, too must study his subject and brood over his experience of it, and make studies in his own medium, though in his case, since he is concerned, in the end, to express not some matter of fact, but an evaluation, the exact record of observation is less essential, and he may more easily rely on unrecorded memory. For the making of his final expression is itself the recording of a continuity of contemplative experience, and its earlier stages are built into the finished product. But in both these cases the recording of experience is incidental to a special intention; it is a means to an end and it is therefore highly selective in terms of relevance to the end in view. In both cases, too, the intention involves an elimination of the temporal reference; for the scientist seeks an eternal law—the discovery of a general pattern in events which recurs *ad infinitum* without change; while the artist isolates his object as an eternal value, and seeks to make it a possession for ever.

There is therefore need for a reflective discipline, the intention of which is neither to generalize nor to particularize but to record. This discipline is history, the business of which is to construct an adequate and reliable public memory. It would be wrong, or at least misleading, to say that the historian is concerned to construct the record of past events. For he is not concerned with events as such, in the scientist's sense. He does not abstract from experience a purely 'objective' world of events. He is concerned with events only as they enter into human experience, and so modify human action; only with the material world or the world of Nature so far as they provide the field of human activity and set the practical problems which men must solve. History is, then, essentially personal; and it exhibits the form of the personal: for it concentrates upon practical activities and treats the reflective achievements of an epoch as secondary and derivative; as of interest in so far as they enter into and condition the practical doings of the time. And since history is concerned with the human past in its pastness, it makes no reference to the future; it does not seek to derive from the past anything that can be referred to the future. This can be best expressed by reference to memory; for memory provides the archetypal form of all historical reflection. The ideal of history is to represent the whole human past as if it were the memory-content of a single agent who had experienced it all, and whose memory was completely adequate and reliable. This ideal explains, among other things, the selectivity of history; by which I mean the way in which the representation of a past epoch varies from historian to historian and from one generation of historians to the next. This variability has led to the view that history is necessarily, and not merely accidentally, coloured by the personal prejudices and interests of the individual who writes it; and therefore is an art rather than a science, inherently subjective. In fact it is merely the 'public' form of one of the functional characteristics of memory. The 'content' of memory is not all present to consciousness at once, it is merely available when required. What requires that this or that aspect or element in memory should be recalled is always a present and practical interest. For what is actively remembered is *ipso facto* brought into a determining relation to present intentions and preoccupations. What is actually recalled is selected for its relevance to the present; and the accounts that we give of the same experience of our own from time to time necessarily vary with the occasion for their production. Nor does this variation necessarily affect their validity. Just as there can be no definitive memory, so there can be no definitive history.

As in all forms of reflection, the ideal determines the methodology of the historian. The raw material of his activity is records, that is to say, published memories. He estimates their reliability and collates them, and so builds up a composite picture which is more reliable than any of the sources taken singly. There are, of course, gaps, and these must be filled in; if possible by the discovery of further records, or if these are not available by inference and imaginative construction, which will be tested and verified in every possible fashion. The results are 'histories': themselves records to be compared and collated with the 'records' produced by other historians. So the co-operative process of reflection moves gradually in the direction of its ideal; towards a single reliable and complete record of human activity in the past, which links the past to the present in a continuity of action, and provides a public memory available to everyone.

This underlying conception of a continuity of human action interests us particularly at the moment. History is not mere chronicle; it is understanding. Its fixed point of reference is the present; its effort is to exhibit the continuity of the past with the present, and the present as continuing the past. But this past is a human past; its elements are the doings of agents. Consequently, its continuity with the present can only be a continuity of action; and action is constituted by intention. Historical understanding is, then, a comprehension of the continuity of human intention, and so far as it succeeds, it exhibits a multitude of individual acts as constituting a single action, in virtue of a community of intention. It is clearly impossible to analyse or expound this complex concept without facing the problem which we have reserved for future consideration—the relatedness of persons in action. We can only notice here, where we are concerned with its empirical employment by the historian, that it presents him with two interrelated problems. He must discover and express the unity of intention which combines the contemporary doings of many agents into the action of one society of agents; and also the continuity of this common intentionality from generation to generation. As an example of the first we might recall our habit of speaking of a battle as an action; of the second the idea of the continuity of British foreign policy in the Nineteenth Century. In both cases we are dealing with many actions of many individuals which constitute a unity of action because they are informed by community and continuity of intention. We must bear in mind, if we are to understand this aright, that intention is not to be confused with end, or a common intention with a common end, or a continuity of intention with the persistence of a determinate end. Intention determines itself progressively in action.

However we are to interpret this, we can at least recognize it as a postulate or working hypothesis of historical reflection. Without intention there is no action; and therefore nothing for history to record; without a unity of continuing action, which is made up of the actions of many agents, it must be impossible to talk sensibly about the acts of a group or a nation or about the policy of a government. An ant-hill or a herd of elephants has no history. Without memory, which is his immediate knowledge of his own past, the individual cannot act; and it is the continuity of memory which combines all his actions into the unity of a single human life. So without a common memory there can be no common action; without a public memory no public life. And without the systematic and methodical investigation of the historian, determining the record of the past in terms of a distinction between true and false, there can be no reliable public memory, but only a legendary tradition.

There are two reasons for introducing such a commentary upon history at this stage of our argument. The first is that it completes—so far as it can be complete at present—our study of reflection and its relation to action. Historical reflection is the matrix of all modes of reflection. They arise from it and return to it again. Without the record of past activity they are impossible; and if the record is unreliable, they are led astray. Memory is the *sine qua non* of personal existence in any of its modes; and an unreliable memory is a fruitful source of faulty action. The consideration of history might well have taken precedence in our study of reflection. We have left it to the last because, when we seek to understand historical reflection, we find ourselves faced with the necessity of analysing the relation of persons in action. This points directly to the subject of our second volume. The other reason is that in history we find, in empirical use, the thought of an intentional unity of actions in one action. If now we take this empirical concept from the historian, and isolate it as a logical form, we reach the point where we must consider what may be called, for want of a better term, the metaphysic of action.

The very mention of metaphysics is apt to arouse feelings of suspicion, more or less violent and hostile, among an influential section of contemporary philosophers. A short comment on this attitude is therefore desirable in order to clarify our own position. The doctrine that metaphysical statements are meaningless has its roots in the positivistic aspect of the Critical philosophy. The ground of this judgement is that a metaphysical assertion cannot be verified, because it purports to refer beyond the limits of possible experience. For Kant, synthetic judgements *a priori* can be known to be true only if they are purely formal. For modern positivists, the formal judgements to which Kant refers are not synthetic but analytic, and their validity is guaranteed by the fact that they are tautological. This difference of doctrine is unimportant in the present connexion; since in either case it rules out the possibility of metaphysics in the sense of the term with which we are concerned. Now this rejection of metaphysics seems entirely justified from the standpoint of the primacy of the theoretical. If the 'I think' is the primary postulate of all knowledge, then metaphysical assertions are meaningless, because they require verification and cannot be verified. But this conclusion is valid *only* on the assumption that the theoretical standpoint is the only possible standpoint. If this is not so, then the conclusion may be taken as a *reductio ad absurdum* of that standpoint. Now we have already shown that the 'Cogito' is inadequate and even self-contradictory as an absolute presupposition of experience; and we have been exploring the possibility of substituting for it the 'I do' of an experience which is primarily practical. Consequently, the possibility of metaphysics remains an open question, and the arguments against its possibility have lost their cogency.

The issue now turns upon the nature of verification. For we must grant, it seems, that any assertion which requires verification, yet does not admit of verification, is meaningless; and any assertion which is reasonably doubted requires verification. From the standpoint which we have adopted, the weakness of the positivist case lies in a misunderstanding of verification; a misunderstanding which is inevitable if theoretical activity is taken to be self-contained and self-sufficient. On this presupposition verification must take the form of a reference from one aspect of reflective experience to another; that is to say, to sense-perception. But a reference to sense perception *as such*—that is to say, as a pure receptivity of the mind,—verifies nothing. It only seems to do so on the assumption that what is given in sense-perception exists independently in its own right. We have already characterized the realist assertion that this is the case as a mere dogma. But it is a groundless assertion only upon his own presuppositions. If sense-perception is taken as an element in action, and not in reflection, the case is different. For then the reference in verification is not to sense-perception, but to action, in which, of course, sense-perception is a constitutive element; and verification is itself the testing of theory in action.

Now it follows from this that the field of verification is much wider than is commonly allowed. For in principle, wherever a reflective construction can enter into the determination of an intention it can be verified. What is required is simply an expectation in action which can be falsified in the event. What is expected may, of course, be a certain perceptual experience. But clearly it need not be. A reflective valuation, as we have noticed already, can equally be verified in action. Then why not a metaphysical assertion? To say that it is meaningless could only signify that whether it was believed or not could make no difference to the intentionality of an agent. There may be assertions of this kind, though I cannot think of any which could be taken seriously. If there are such assertions, then I, for one, will happily agree that they are meaningless. But most metaphysical assertions, at least those which have been seriously maintained, are not of this kind. They are assertions which, if seriously believed, make a profound difference to the direction of human intentions. The differential consequences of the kinds of action which they promote constitute their verification. For to act upon a belief involves expectations which may or may not be falsified in the event. What is expected may not be a particular sensory experience. Indeed if the belief is a metaphysical one it clearly cannot be. It must be remembered that even in science to verify a hypothesis does not mean to demonstrate its truth. No hypothesis can ever be established beyond the possibility of revision. What verification does is to provide practical grounds for believing an assertion, in preference to any known alternative. Belief is a practical category; to justify a belief is to provide rational grounds for acting on the assumption that it is true. Since we cannot pursue the question how metaphysical beliefs are tested in action, I shall add only one further remark. If we can understand, to whatever extent, what difference would be made in our intention if we acted in the belief that a certain proposition were true, then that proposition has a meaning: and if the meaning of a proposition is its verification, in some sense of this obscure phrase, then the mode of verification to which it is susceptible is a clue to its interpretation.

The particular metaphysical assertion which I have in mind is that the world is one action. This is the conclusion to which our whole argument moves, and it has been implicit from the beginning. For to think the Self as agent is to think the unity of the world as a unity of action. We can therefore draw this series of lectures suitably to a close by making this conclusion formally explicit.

If we take our stand, as the philosophical tradition does, on the 'I think', and conceive the Self as subject, then any attempt to think the unity of the Real must conceive it as object of knowledge. This, we have seen, necessitates a dualism. The Self and its activities or states cannot be included in the world which is known. The theoretical alternative is to include the Object within the Subject, so that in the last analysis the Subject is its own object and all knowledge is self-consciousness. This is the conclusion of Objective Idealism; but it is solipsistic, and there-fore self-refuting. For solipsism is an ultimate denial of the possibility of any distinction between true and false, and so of the possibility of knowledge. In that case it cannot itself be true or false and is merely meaningless.

Now dualism is the denial of the possibility of thinking a unity of the Real. The world divides into an absolute duality of objective and subjective; only the objective is real; while the subjective is unreal. To think the world as a whole would be to think it as a completely determinate object. But such a concept is necessarily exclusive; we have considered it already in the form of the concept of the continuant, and have seen that it is an ideal abstraction within our experience of the world, an isolate which falls within the whole. It excludes from reality all that is indeterminate; therefore all error, all illusion, and all possibility of action. But indeterminateness is an essential character of the Self, whether as subject knowing or as agent in action. In knowing the Self determines an object theoretically; in acting it determines the future practically. If nothing real is indeterminate, then neither action nor knowledge is possible, and the existence of the Self is illusory; there is, in fact, no self. In so far, then, as metaphysics involves the endeavour to think the world as a whole, including in the world ourselves and our experience of the world, metaphysics, on the basis of the primacy of the theoretical, is an impossibility. The result could only be a dualism of real and unreal, which in the nature of the case must issue in antinomies.

All this is no more than a *resumé* of previous conclusions. But we discovered also that when we substituted the 'I do' for the 'I think', and carried on our reflection from the standpoint of action, there emerged a new logical form which we called the form of the personal. We defined it as the form of a unity in which the positive included its own negative as a necessary constituent. By means of this form we were able to overcome the dualism of subjective and objective, of mind and matter, and to give an account of action. Now if this form is given a metaphysical use, it will enable us to think the determinate as necessarily including its negative, the indeterminate; or, more generally, to think Reality as constituted by the inclusion of the unreal in its own being. Such a concept would then enable us to think the unity of the world without falling into dualism and antinomy.

We have accepted, so far, the *prima facie* distinction between actions and events; between what is done and what happens. We have now to ask whether this distinction constitutes another dualism. If it does, then it is impossible to think a unity of the world, and the understanding must confine itself within limits; coming to a halt in face of questions which, as Kant said, it cannot help but ask, yet cannot hope to answer. If it does not, then one of the terms of the distinction must ultimately reduce to the other. The alternatives are that we should think reality either as a unity of events or as a unity of actions; that is to say, either as one *process* or as one *action*.

Contemporary thought, under the dominant influence of science, does, at least implicitly, conceive the world as a single process; either biologically as an evolutionary process, or mathematically as a material process of events obeying physical laws. But we are in a position to reject this alternative decisively. For we have seen that the conception of a unity of events, whether conceived physically or organically, is the conception of the continuant, and that the continuant is an ideal abstraction from our experience as agents. It is constituted by the exclusion of action. This concept of process cannot therefore include action as an element in the unity it seeks to express. If the world is a unitary process, it must be a world in which nothing is ever done; in which everything simply happens; a world, then, in which everything is matter of fact and nothing is ever intended. We should have to assert, in that case, that there are no actions; that what seem such are really events. It will not be sufficient to say that all our actions are determined; for this is a contradiction in terms. The capacity to act is freedom; what has to be denied, if the world is one event, is that anything is ever intended. But in that case the assertion itself must be unintentional, and therefore meaningless. In rejecting this alternative, we are merely using the criterion that we established earlier, that since the 'I do' is the primary certainty, any theory which explicitly or implicitly denies it must be false.

On the other hand, we have seen that the concept of action includes the concept of the continuant process as its own negative. Any action, in its actuality, if we abstract from its intentionality, and so from the knowledge which directs it, presents itself as a process of events. In reflection, once it is done, it can be described exhaustively as matter of fact, without reference to the intention which determined it. It follows from this that what appears to us to be a process of events which happen in a necessary succession may always be a part or an aspect of an action. Granted that in our empirical experience we must recognize occurrences which we cannot refer to the intention of an agent, and which we must treat as mere happenings, it still does not follow that they are not so referable. If we cannot prove intention from premisses that are matter of observed fact, neither can we disprove it. It is therefore *possible* to think the world as one action. It is *not possible* to think it as a unitary process.

It is then logically impossible that the world should be a single process; it is logically possible that it should be one action. But this does not prove anything actual. We must therefore ask whether there is any reason why we should think the unity of the Real at all? In pure theory there is none. But pure theory must mean a reflection which has no reference to action, and which is therefore meaningless. We exist only as agents; and in our existence we are parts of the world, dependent upon it for the support and the resistance which make our action possible. The thought of the world as a unity is a postulate of action. For any action in the world depends on the co-operation of the world. It is indeed an integration of the movements of the Agent with the movements of the Other, so that in action the Self and the Other form a unity. This integration *is* the action and its unity is intentional. It would be impossible unless the process of the Other, independently of the agent's intention, were itself systematic; for if not there would be no ground for any expectation that the movement initiated by the agent would be continued by natural processes, in one way rather than another. If we could not rely upon the world outside us, we could not act in it. We can act only through knowledge of the Other; and only what is a determinable unity can be known. It does not follow, as we have seen, that its future can be completely determined in advance; only that whatever occurs must be systematically related to what has gone before, so that through all its changes the world remains one world.

We must, therefore, as agents, think the world as a unity: and we have seen that this unity can only be coherently thought as a unity of action. This means that we must think the world in which we act, and of which we are constituents, as a unity of intention. But, admittedly, any thought, however formal, requires verification, and the possibility of verification is grounded on the differential effect it has upon intention. If we act as if the world, in its unity, is intentional; that is, if we believe in practice that the world is one action—and our consideration of history has shown us what this signifies—we shall act differently from anyone who does not believe this. We shall act as though our own actions were our contributions to the one inclusive action which is the history of the world. If, on the other hand, we believe that the world is a mere process of events which happen as they happen, we shall act differently. Our conception of the unity of the world determines a way of life; and the satisfactoriness or unsatisfactoriness of that way of life is its verification.

The heart of this verification must lie in the effect of the belief upon the relations of persons; and only when we have considered this topic will it be possible to go beyond the formality of our present conclusion. Meanwhile, in bringing to a close the first stage of our inquiry, we may profitably return to our starting-point. The long argument of modern philosophy, we said, has moved steadily in the direction of an atheistic conclusion; and with it the historical development of our civilization has moved towards irreligion. At the same time this has precipitated a revolutionary crisis in society, and made a break in the philosophical tradition which compels us to start afresh from a revision of its fundamental assumption, the primacy of the theoretical. We have substituted the 'I do' for the 'I think', and made a first tentative effort to follow out the implications of this radical modification. Very much remains obscure; but there is one result which is sufficiently clear. The argument which starts from the primacy of the practical moves steadily in the direction of a belief in God. To think the world in practical terms is ultimately to think the unity of the world as one action, and therefore as informed by a unifying intention.

THE WORLD AS ONE ACTION

It may, indeed, prove possible to think the process of the world as intentional without thinking a supreme Agent whose act the world is. But *prima facie*, at least, it is not possible to do so. The conflict between religion and atheism turns, in large part at least, on the issue whether the process of the world is intentional or not. We noticed, in our first chapter, that contemporary existentialism, in its division into theist and atheist wings, poses the substantial problem of philosophy in our day in the alternatives, 'God or Nothing'. We may now add to this, as a pointer to the direction of a verification, that the theistic alternative issues in the hope of an ultimate unity of persons in fellowship, which gives meaning to human effort; while atheist existentialism finds human relationship an insoluble problem and all human projects doomed to frustration and ultimate meaninglessness. As Sartre says in *Huis clos*, '*L'enfer, c'est les autres*'.

Index

INDEX

Behaviour, psychology, 38
  understanding of, 116
Behaviourism, 125
Belief, in freedom, 57
  and doubt, 76
  and knowledge, 78
  and verification, 216, 221
Berkeley, 78
Bio-chemistry, biology, 34
Biology, bio-physics, 61
  and modern philosophy, 31–34
Browning, *Abt Vogler*, 42

Cartesianism, Kant, 39
  Hamann, 72
Categories of the understanding, 50
Causality, application, 118
  relation to action, 151
  self-contradictory conception, 152
  and agency, 160, 165
Certainty, logical and psychological, 76
Character, and habit, 196
  and motive, 198
Christendom, Western, 26
Christianity, guardian of the personal, 30
City state, 25
Coenasthesia, 113
Cogito, 50
  Kant, 73, 74
  meaning of, 80
Collingwood, R. G., 153 n.
Communication, speech and thought, 74
  and expression, 187
Communism, 30
Comte, A., 36
Concepts, understanding, 49
  empirical, 49
  pure concept, 49, 178
Concrete individual, 176
Consciousness, as motive, 119
  limits of, 120
  organic, 125
Contemplative knowledge, 200

Contingency, 148
Continuant, and human activities, 161
  and the object world, 171
Copernican revolution, 85
Critical philosophy, 39, 53, 74
  and Romantics, 43, 62
  the Cartesian period, 62
  inconsistency of, 68
  adequacy of, 70
  religion, 70
  logical empiricism, 73
Critique, *of Practical Reason*, 40, 53, 70
  Third, 42, 58
  of Pure Reason, 43, 53, 68
  of religion, 72–73

Data of intuition, 50
Deity, conception of, 17
Democracy, 29
Descartes, R., 19, 27, 28, 32, 50, 74–75, 79, 80, 81, 104
  appeal from authority to reason, 75
Determinism, 135
Dialectic, form of thought, 34
  and biology, 34
  Critique of Pure Reason, 40, 72
  of illusion, 43
  idealism and Hegel, 53
Dimensions of action, 128
Discursive thought, 51
  Hamann's attack, 46
Dogmatism, 17
Doubt, rejection of authority, 75
  and belief, 76
  as a method, 77
Dreaming, and self-developing ideas, 172
Dualism, 79, 217
  cogito, 73
  kinds of, 73
  genesis of, 117
  and the theoretical standpoint, 178

INDEX

INDEX

INDEX

Memory, and imagination, 208
  and observation, 209
  its inadequacy, 209
  public memory, 210
  metaphysics, 27
  and the dialectic of reason, 53
  its reflection, 214
  verification through action, 216
  totality, 218
Mind, creative spontaneity, 32
  mind-body problem, 79
Morality, art, 53
  aesthetics, 54
  praxis, 55
  evil, 99
Moral judgement, infallibility, 140
Moral law, freedom, 65
  St. Paul, 70
Motive, distinguished from intention, 194–5, 197
  motive consciousness, 195
  and feeling, 196, 197
  positive and negative motivation, 196

Natural law, Other as continuant, 154
  generality, 164
Natural theology, 17
  idea of, 17–18
Nature, Herder's notion, 40, 58
  Kant, 50
  as work of art, 60
  as organic, 144
  Laws, 156, 157
Newton, Isaac, method, 131
  first law of Motion, 143, 155
  law of gravitation, 135
Noumenal world, 46
  science and morality, 64

Object, its determination, 49
  subject, 51
  objective awareness, 167–8
Objective idealism, 42, 217
  Critical philosophy, 62

Organic evolution, 34
  and history, 205
  and the liberal faith, 206
Organism, concept of, 33
  form of movement, 119
  teleological behaviour, 149
Other, God as, 18
  and Will, 109
  as continuant, 144

Particular, 176
Past, as continuant, 170–1
  the object of reflection, 208
Perception, standpoint of agent, 104 ff
  discrimination of the Other, 197
Person, concept of, 118
Personal, the form of, 17, 37
  crisis of, 29
  intellectual form of, 29
  values, 29
  and Christianity, 30
  communication, 74
Phenomenology, 26
Philosophy, history of, 19
  Western, 23
  as a way of life, 24
  ancient, 25
  tradition, 25 f.
  modern, 31
  science, 31 f.
  organic and personal, 37
  organic development, 62
  coherence, 66
Philosophy of history, 60
Physical sciences, 22
Physics and habit, 163
Planning, nature of, 83
Plato, 99
  Theaetetus, 99
Power, as means, 182
Practical determination, and time, 133
Practical, Primacy of the, rejection of dualism, 84
  and the antinomy of freedom, 134

227

INDEX

INDEX

229